T0305289

Credit and Crisis from Marx to Minsky

Credit and Crisis from Marx to Minsky

Jan Toporowski

Professor of Economics and Finance, SOAS University of London, UK, Visiting Professor of Economics and Finance, International University College, Turin, and Visiting Professor of Economics, University of Bergamo, Italy

Edward Elgar
PUBLISHING

Cheltenham, UK • Northampton, MA, USA

Published by
Edward Elgar Publishing Limited
The Lypiatts
15 Lansdown Road
Cheltenham
Glos GL50 2JA
UK

Edward Elgar Publishing, Inc.
William Pratt House
9 Dewey Court
Northampton
Massachusetts 01060
USA

A catalogue record for this book
is available from the British Library

Library of Congress Control Number: 2020942915

This book is available electronically in the **Elgar**online
Economics subject collection
http://dx.doi.org/10.4337/9781788972154

ISBN 978 1 78897 214 7 (cased)
ISBN 978 1 78897 215 4 (eBook)

Printed by CPI Group (UK) Ltd, Croydon CR0 4YY

Contents

Introduction

'Authors write their own history, but they do not write it just as they please; they do not write it under circumstances chosen by themselves ...'

In 2005 my book *Theories of Financial Disturbance* was published. It had originally been conceived as an extended introductory literature review to my book *The End of Finance* (Routledge 2000). *The End of Finance* was supposed to show the structural interconnections between: capital markets, dominated by pension funds and insurance companies, and kept liquid, inflated and deflated by credit inflows and outflows; pension funds, whose balance between surpluses and deficits turns the capital markets into, essentially, Ponzi financing structures; and financial derivatives that are supposed to provide stability to non-financial users of financial markets, but the derivatives themselves succumb to unstable demand and supply. *Theories of Financial Disturbance* was intended to show the origins and antecedents of these ideas in the work of Adam Smith, who believed that unregulated interest rates would cause 'prodigals and projectors' (what we would now call spendthrifts and entrepreneurs) to 'crowd out' sound businesses from the credit system with their extravagance and speculations. *Theories of Financial Disturbance* then explains how Adam Smith's views on usury were eventually abandoned in the nineteenth century as laissez-faire spread to banking and central banks needed to use interest rate policy to regulate gold reserves.

Theories of Financial Disturbance went on to describe the evolution through the twentieth century of ideas on how banking and finance may disturb the capitalist economy through the works of Thorstein Veblen, Rosa Luxemburg, Ralph Hawtrey, John Maynard Keynes, Irving Fisher, Michał Kalecki, Josef Steindl, John Kenneth Galbraith, Charles Kindleberger, and Hyman Minsky. The justification for this selection was a three-fold classification of theories of banking and finance. *Equilibrium* theories of banking and finance are ones that show these activities to be part of a general equilibrium together with the 'real', or non-financial, economy. In a general equilibrium no judgement may be made about causes of economic disturbances, since these may come from a change in any of the financial or real parts of the economy. Since most finance theories use a general equilibrium method of some kind, they thereby exclude the possibility of macroeconomic disturbance arising from the financial sector.

A second category of theory is what I called *reflective* theories. In these theories financial disturbances merely reflect underlying problems, difficulties, disequilibria, or 'contradictions' in the non-financial economy. This is epitomised in much Marxist writing that regards the state of the financial markets as merely reflecting conditions in the 'real' economy, class struggles, changes in rates of profit and so on. But similar views may be found among some finance theorists who regard financial markets as driven by firm or market 'fundamentals', e.g. the 'Efficient Market' theory of Eugene Fama. In these theories banking and finance do not play an active part in determining activity in the real economy, but merely supply credit to non-financial activities that create their own crises and disequilibria.

Finally, there are *critical theories of finance* in which credit plays an active part in disturbing the non-financial economy. The theories described in this book are all attempts to show how finance can do this.

In my *Theories of Financial Disturbance* I also gave an account of some of the authors that I had excluded from consideration in that book. The most prominent group of these authors were theorists of the business cycle, pioneered by Knut Wicksell, but also Joseph Schumpeter, John A. Hobson, Friedrich von Hayek and Karl Polanyi. Finance is given a key part in their theories, most notably in the work of Schumpeter and Hobson. However, in the end, their business cycle analyses were driven by non-financial factors, in particular excessive saving, or over-investment, combined with, in the case of Hayek, inappropriate monetary policy, rather than influences emanating systematically from the financial markets. A second group of authors omitted from my book were 'monetary reformers' those such as C.H. ('Major') Douglas and Silvio Gesell. Together with Hobson and Polanyi they viewed finance as a critical flaw in capitalism. But they lacked a systematic analysis that is necessary to explain the working out of those flaws and specifically to show the mechanisms by which they create problems for the economy at large. Much the same is true of the more recent, New Keynesian, analyses of Ben Bernanke and Mark Gertler or the theory of 'rational' bubbles (Bernanke and Gertler 1989; Bikhchandani et al. 1992) or other attempts to model financial disequilibrium (e.g. Allen and Gale 2004). These show the *possibility* of disequilibrium, under certain specific assumptions, rather than a systematic account of the functioning of finance in the capitalist economy.

In any case, too many of these authors take their concept of 'disturbance' from the period of 'classic' capitalism, in the first half of the nineteenth century, when capitalists financed their ventures largely with short-term borrowing, and the possibilities of matching the maturity financial liabilities, through long-term finance, to the maturity of productive assets, were limited. These authors therefore built models around a concept of a financial crisis as essentially a banking crisis of maturity mismatch. By contrast the development of capital markets inaugurated a different, more macroeconomic and structural kind of financial crisis. Unfortunately, the academic discussion of financial stability has not kept up with *structural* changes in financial systems, which have altered financial processes and the way in which financial disturbances proceed. There may be a reason why a general theory of financial crisis should include the banking crises of 'classic capitalism'. But to restrict consideration of financial crisis to such banking crises is a display of ignorance rather than understanding. My original distinction between 'equilibrium', 'reflective' and 'critical' theories of finance was perhaps something over-simplified, or perhaps represents a first approximation only. My more recent research suggests a more evolutionary distinction in which financial systems have progressed over time, with corresponding changes in debt structures and crisis mechanisms.[1]

Since the publication of *Theories of Financial Disturbance* a major financial crisis has emerged in the United States and Great Britain, and has since weighed heavily on the economies of North America and Europe. The obvious role of finance and debt in this crisis has boosted interest in ways in which the credit system may disturb capitalist economies. For the most part this latest crisis remains interpreted as a banking problem, whether of maturity transformation or asymmetric information. Its broader macroeconomic consequences have been highlighted in a new set of theories of 'financialisation'[2]. These rest on a mass of evidence of the growing activity in financial markets and expanding financial income. To date financialisation theories largely treat such financial activity and income as an usurious burden on the rest of the economy, rather than providing new insight into the macroeconomic functioning of finance.[3] It is with a view to deepening this literature that I have revised and extended my earlier book.

These chapters can be read separately or altogether, if the reader is willing to tolerate a certain amount of repetition. This tolerant reader, if sufficiently alert, will pick up the hints in this book at the most recent conclusions to which these reflections have led me, namely Kalecki's monetary theory, and a pure monetary theory of interest that requires portfolio liquidity, but not the production of a current surplus against the gross amount of debt in the economy. As Kalecki pointed out, capitalists may be presumed to have money, and this makes them independent of current sales revenues, at least in their management of financial operations. Kalecki's monetary theory points the way to a final break with the classical theory of interest that has prevailed in economics since David Ricardo, and ties the rate of interest to the rate of profit.[4]

Theories of Financial Disturbance was completed in circumstances of professional crisis for its author, under pressure to complete a Leverhulme Fellowship project. A further reason for revisiting my survey of critics of finance was because the accounts of two key thinkers, Karl Marx and Hyman Minsky, that were given in that book were less than satisfactory. In the case of Karl Marx, I have largely changed my earlier view that his was a 'reflective' approach to finance. I owe this change to my discussions with Riccardo Bellofiore, and my reading of Tadeusz Kowalik's classic work on Rosa Luxemburg.[5] Those discussions and that reading have also contributed to the more extensive and deeper understanding of the work of Hyman Minsky that is now in this new volume. The whole volume has also benefited from research for the Financialization, Economy, Society and Sustainable Development project, financed under the FP7 programme by the European Commission.

Earlier drafts of some of these chapters have appeared as 'Marx's *Grundrisse* and the Monetary Business Cycle' in R. Bellofiore, G. Starosta and P.D. Thomas (eds.) *In Marx's Laboratory Critical interpretations of the Grundrisse* Leiden: Brill 2013; 'Rosa Luxemburg and Finance' in R. Bellofiore (ed.) *Rosa Luxemburg and the Critique of Political Economy* London: Routledge 2009, pp. 81–91; 'The Kalecki-Steindl Theory of Financial Fragility' in J. Toporowski and Ł. Mamica (eds.) *Michał Kalecki in the 21st Century* Basingstoke: Palgrave Macmillan 2014, pp. 252–264; 'The Monetary Theory of Kalecki and Minsky' *Working Papers* No. 172, Department of Economics, The School of Oriental and African Studies, University of London, March 2012, ISSN 1753-5816 (Polish translation as 'Minsky'ego i Kaleckiego teoria pieniądza' in K. Łaski and J. Osiatyński (eds.) *Globalny kryzys gospodarczy po roku 2008. Perspektywa postkeynesowska* Warszawa:

Instytut Studiów Zaawansowanych 2015); 'Henry Simons and the Other Minsky Moment' *Studi e Note di Economia* Anno XV. N. 3-2010, December 2010, pp. 363–368. These papers have all been revised to integrate them within this book.

A second exposition of critical theories of finance in modern capitalism extends the intellectual debts outstanding from the first exposition, without diminishing any individual debt. Among those who have helped me are Riccardo Bellofiore, Stephanie Blankenburg, Victoria Chick, David Cobham, Andy Denis, Sheila Dow, Gary Dymski, Charles Goodhart, David Gowland, Joseph Halevi, Geoff Harcourt, Peter Howells, Susan Howson, Jesper Jesperson, John King, Peter Kriesler, David Laidler, Julio Lopez-Gallardo, Tracy Mott, Geert Reuten, Geoff Tily and Randy Wray. The saddest debts are those that can only be repaid to memory of the departed Warren Samuels, Nina Shapiro, Tadeusz Kowalik, Kazimierz Łaski and Zvi Schloss. A very special debt is owed to Noemi Levy-Orlik and her students who have participated in the formation of this book since the first idea for it emerged some two decades ago. I have also benefited from the interest of some brilliant younger scholars, Jo Michell, Daniela Tavasci, Luigi Ventimiglia, Ewa Karwowski, Jennifer Churchill, Mimoza Shabani, Jago Penrose, Hanna Szymborska and Robert Jump. Robert Jump, in particular, has been very generous in putting together these chapters into a logical structure and a draft on which I could work.

Most present of all is the inspiration of Anita Prażmowska, and the dedication of Miriam Prażmowska-Toporowska.

NOTES

1. Toporowski 2020.
2. Stockhammer 2012.
3. Michell and Toporowski (2013–2014).
4. This is further explained in Toporowski (2019).
5. Kowalik 2014.

PART I

Capitalism and financial crisis

1. Marx and the monetary business cycle

In the course of developing the ideas that were to become his comprehensive study of capitalist economic relations and dynamics in *Capital*, Marx had to confront the commonly observed coincidence of economic slump with banking crisis. This had given rise to a conviction that economic crisis was caused by the mismanagement of the monetary system. This view had become common among political economists and critics of capitalism with the emergence of more or less regular business cycles since the early nineteenth century. The key, therefore, to stabilisation of capitalist production and trade is a reform of the monetary system. It remains common today, uniting conservatives with some of capitalism's bitterest critics. Marx confronted these ideas in a first attempt at a comprehensive analysis of capitalism, his *Grundrisse der Kritik der Politischen Ökonomie (Rohentwurf)*.[1] This is a work of extraordinary range which allows it to be read in a number of different ways. The first, and probably the most obvious reading, is as a set of preliminary, transitional notes for the work that was to become *Capital*. A second reading that attracted widespread interest when the book was published, was as a philosophical introduction to Marx's critique of political economy, outlining the method that Marx was to use in his economic analysis (or not, according to the followers of Louis Althusser). Not least among the important features of the book, in this author's opinion, is a tantalising fragment, a mere few hundred words, on Greek art.[2]

However, the key to understanding the book is given in the chapter titles. A methodological introduction is followed by a chapter on money, and then a very extensive chapter, that takes up the vast bulk of a very long book, on capital. The purpose of this arrangement is to show that the monetary appearance of objects and relations is illusory, because capital is a social relationship, not a pecuniary one. Hence the phrase that recurs in the titles that Marx gave to his writings on political economy: the *critique* of political economy, rather than *a helpful guide to correct doctrines* in political economy. This accounts for much of the difficulty that arises in reading Marx's writings on political economy. Those works can only be fully understood by first reading the works that Marx was criticising. A first approximation may be obtained by reading the three volumes of *Theories of Surplus Value*. However, the task can be made much simpler by concentrating on a key theme of current significance that occurs in the *Grundrisse* and in *Capital*, namely the role that credit plays in capitalist production and crisis.

The chapter is organised as follows. A first section examines Marx's views on credit as presented in the *Grundrisse*. This is then contrasted, in the second section, with a more mature view on credit cycles, presented in Volume III of *Capital*. A third section argues that the two views are consistent with a historical view of the evolution of finance. A brief conclusion summarises the argument.

1.1 REJECTING THE MONETARY BUSINESS CYCLE ...

The first chapter of the *Grundrisse*, on Money, begins with a quotation from a book, *De la réforme des banques* by Alfred Darimon:

> The root of the evil is the predominance which opinion obstinately assigns to the role of the precious metals in circulation and exchange.

Darimon (1819–1902), a journalist and politician, and follower of social philosopher and critic Pierre Joseph Proudhon, was what Keynes called a 'monetary reformer', i.e. a theorist who argues that the inadequacies of capitalism may be removed by reforming the monetary system. In Darimon's case, the reform he sought was joint stock banking backed by credit insurance. This he believed would provide the flexible credit supply that would prevent the financial crises that plagued France (and Britain) in the first half of the nineteenth century as a result of the use of precious metals to back bank credit.

Marx proceeded to castigate Darimon for his weak understanding of bank credit: 'he completely identifies *monetary turnover* with *credit*'. (In an aside that could be addressed to certain twenty-first century Marxist monetary theorists, Marx went on to remark 'The notion of *crédit gratuit*, incidentally, is only a hypocritical, philistine and anxiety-ridden form of the saying: property is theft. Instead of the workers *taking* the capitalists' capital, the capitalists are supposed to be compelled to *give* it to them'.)[3]

Marx identified 'the fundamental question' as:

> Can the existing relations of production and the relations of distribution which
> correspond to them be revolutionised by a change in the instrument of cir-
> culation, in the organisation of circulation? ... Various forms of money may
> correspond better to social production at various stages; one form may remedy
> evils against which another is powerless; but none of them, as long as they
> remain forms of money, and as long as money remains an essential relation of
> production, is capable of overcoming the contradictions inherent in the money
> relation, and can instead only hope to reproduce these contradictions in one or
> another form. One form of wage labour may correct the abuses of another, but
> no form can correct abuse of wage labour itself.[4]

Marx's argument was essentially that crises occur because of contradictions in production and exchange, rather than in the medium of
exchange: The 'bullion drains' (loss of gold from the banking system)
that cause financial crises are themselves the results of changes in real,
non-monetary, factors such as 'domestic harvest failures in a chief food
crop (e.g. grain), crop failure abroad and hence increased prices in
one of the main imported consumer goods (e.g. tea) ... crop failure in
industrial raw materials (cotton, wool silk, flax etc.), excessive imports
(caused by speculation, war etc.) ...' with the consequence that 'a part of
(the nation's) invested capital or labour is not reproduced – real loss of
production'.[5]

Marx then went on to argue that money prices could not measure the
true price of commodities, but 'labour money denominated in labour
time would ... equate the *real value* (exchange value) of commodities'.[6]
This early Marx reappears in Emile Zola's extraordinary novelistic
treatment of financial crisis, *L'Argent*, as the 'Karl Marxite' Sigismund
Busch, devoting his dying years to the calculation of a system of prices
that would correspond to labour time, and that would therefore eliminate exploitation. This endeavour was then revived by those Marxian
economists who have devoted themselves to the solution of the so-called
'transformation problem'.[7]

The remainder of the chapter is devoted to contrasting and criticising
the presumed intrinsic value of precious metals, as opposed to the social
character of capitalist production and hence prices. This is therefore the
prelude to Marx's very long chapter on capital.

1.2   ... ONLY TO EMBRACE THE MONETARY BUSINESS CYCLE ...

There is no doubt that the chapter on money is inadequate. It is unsystematic, consisting of notes that break off inconclusively, and arguments criss-crossed with Marx's invective against Darimon, extended to Saint-Simonians such as Isaac Pereire.[8] A serious gap in Marx's argument is the absence of any general account of economic or financial crisis. As indicated above, Marx suggested that crises were caused by real factors, disrupting production, but that the causes of any given financial crisis were particular to that crisis.

This lacuna was made up less than a decade later when Marx drafted Volume III of *Capital*. In this volume he introduced corporate finance into his argument in the guise of 'interest-bearing capital', a separate kind of money capital that emerges to finance production.[9] This allowed Marx to distinguish between bank crises, caused by 'bullion drains' and problems that arise with refinancing industrial credit, or 'interest-bearing capital'. These problems arise because industrial credit is put into production. At this point the industrial capitalist no longer has the money, obtained when the credit was advanced, with which to repay that credit. That money had been used to buy means of production, the revenue from which is insufficient for immediate repayment of the credit advanced.[10]

In modern terminology, the process of production and (real) capital accumulation requires the purchase of illiquid assets using credit. This was identified as a feature of a Keynesian theory of crisis by Hyman P. Minsky:

> The process of selling financial assets or liabilities to fulfill cash-payment commitments is called 'position-making' the position being the unit's holdings of assets which, while they earn income, do not possess markets in which they can be readily sold. For corporations the 'position' which has to be financed is the capital assets necessary for production; for financial firms, the 'position' is defined by the assets with poor secondary markets ... the owners of (industrial) capital-assets speculate by debt-financing investment and positions in the stock of capital-assets ...

Such firms 'with elaborated liability structures develop cash payment commitments which exceed the cash receipts they will get over the short period from contracts they own, or from operations. To fulfill their cash-payment commitments, they must refinance by selling either their assets or their liabilities.'[11]

1.3   ... MAY BE DONE DIALECTICALLY

There is a functionalist tendency among Marxist economists whose common weakness consists of illicitly generalising from some logical necessity of a particular model of capitalism. In one version of this, all capitalist phenomena are treated as somehow 'functional' for capitalism which, by implication, is deemed incapable of operating in an inefficient, or dysfunctional, way. This kind of analysis appeals to critics of capitalism who would hang their critiques on the obvious 'unfairness' of capitalism, or the seemingly intractable poverty existing in capitalist societies. Monetary and financial theory, in this kind of functionalism, emerges from an examination of the monetary and financing needs of capitalist production and exchange, and serves those needs logically because money and credit have no other function in the capitalist economy. (Examples of this kind of reasoning may be found most famously in Hilferding's *Finance Capital*, and, more recently, in the 'circuitist' theory of money, or among the contributions to Moseley 2005.) In another, weaker, version of this functionalism, the institutions of a capitalist society are judged according to how they contribute to the efficient functioning of the capitalist economy. This is notable in the French Regulationist school, or among their transatlantic intellectual cousins, the Social Structure of Accumulation school of American Marxists.

This functionalist approach does not really do full justice to Marx's historic dialectic which explains the apparent paradox of his rejection of any monetary business cycle in the *Grundrisse* only to embrace it in Volume III of *Capital*. In the earlier work, Marx was concerned to show that monetary relations could not explain capitalism, or be the foundation for it as a historical formation. In Volume III of *Capital* he showed how the need to finance industrial production brought about the historical emergence of 'interest-bearing capital'.[12] The unjustly neglected Marxist monetary theorist Karl Niebyl was to show how the prodigious credit needs of factory production induced the financial innovations that came about in the latter half of the nineteenth century with the routine establishment of companies capable of issuing long-term financial liabilities.[13]

At first glance, Marx's and Niebyl's approaches are 'functionalist' in the sense that credit markets develop to satisfy the financing requirements of capitalist production. Industrial capitalism pre-dates capitalist financial markets. Hence finance cannot be the social foundation for capitalism, nor, according to the *Grundrisse*, can monetary relations be the ultimate explanation for fluctuations in capitalism as it emerges. The problem with the functionalist view is that finance does not exist just to serve industrial capitalism. If this were so, then the United States would today be an industrial super-power, instead of just a financial and military super-power. The central issue is that, having emerged to serve industrial capitalism, the financial markets then change that capitalism: financial markets become a much more liquid source of profit (if not surplus value: the squeeze imposed by high interest rates on the residual surplus value of the industrial capitalist, a jejune problem that belongs, as Marx rightly noted, to early capitalism, rather than our capitalism dominated by finance[14]). Historically interest-bearing capital, with credit inflation, became the means by which capitalism refocused on balance sheet restructuring as a source of cash flow rather than just production. In this way, financial innovation changed the nature and the financing needs of industrial capital.

The process by which capitalist production induced financial innovation to extend production but, ultimately, to corrupt capitalist production is a historic dialectic that Marx knew well. In his polemic against Lord Overstone, who had argued that interest rates were high because profits were high, Marx put forward the view that higher interest rates may be caused by greater demand for money capital to finance production, which production is then diminished by the higher interest rates. Marx dismissed Overstone in the following terms:

> That anything can ultimately destroy its own cause is a logical absurdity only for the usurer enamoured of the high interest rate. The greatness of the Romans was the cause of their conquests, and their conquests destroyed their greatness. Wealth is the cause of luxury and luxury destroys wealth ...[15]

This logic is well applied to finance: Just because financial markets developed to finance industry does not mean that they remained in this ancillary position, or that they cannot depress capital accumulation or agitate capitalism with credit cycles. Too many Marxists and post-Keynesians share a neo-classical textbook view that is stuck in the primordial function of the financial markets. The radical political economist of finance re-examines the financial markets of today and how they alter the nature and dynamics of capitalism.

1.4   CONCLUSION

In his *Grundrisse* Marx rejected monetary relations as the foundation
and explanation for capitalism. However, monetary relations return
in his theory of crisis, which is a kind of monetary business cycle à la
Minsky. This apparent paradox may be explained by the dialectical role
played by finance in the development of capitalism: The financing needs
of capitalist production induce financial innovation ('interest-bearing
capital') which comes to have a dominant, rather than a subordinate, role
in relation to production. The dominance of finance allows credit cycles
to determine the nature and dynamics of capitalism. Marx himself was to
conclude that:

> The social character of capital is first promoted and wholly realised through
> the full development of the credit and the banking system ... The distribution
> of capital as a special business, a social function, is taken out of the hands of
> the private capitalists and usurers. But at the same time, banking and credit
> thus become the most potent means of driving capitalist production beyond
> its own limits, and one of the most effective vehicles of crises and swindle.[16]

NOTES

1. Marx 1993.
2. Ibid., pp. 110–111.
3. Ibid., p. 123.
4. Ibid.
5. Ibid., p. 127.
6. Ibid., p. 137.
7. Cf. Bellofiore 1989.
8. The banking doctrines of the Saint-Simonians are further discussed in Toporowski 2002, part 1.
9. Marx 1959, part V.
10. Ibid., pp. 488–493.
11. Minsky 1975, pp. 123–124.
12. Marx 1959, chapters XXI and XXV.
13. Niebyl 1946. Engels alludes to this in the brief chapter he wrote on the stock exchange to conclude Volume III of *Capital*.
14. See Marx 1959, pp. 109–110.
15. Ibid., p. 422.
16. Ibid., p. 607.

2. Marx and the emergence of debt markets

2.1 INTEREST-BEARING CAPITAL

In his first attempts at presenting a systematic critique of political economy, in his *Grundrisse* and then in *A Contribution to the Critique of Political Economy*, Marx had been concerned to show how money values and monetary relations were merely the framework for a façade, a framework which determined the appearance but not the reality of the social relations of production in the capitalist economy. Both of those early drafts consist of a chapter on money combined with a chapter indicating the true relations of value in capitalism (a chapter on Capital in the case of the *Grundrisse* and a chapter on the Commodity in the case of the *Contribution*). Marx attempted to give a more systematic account of the role of money in the capitalist economy in the notes and drafts that make up Volume III of *Capital*. Here, the most important section is Part V on the 'Division of Profit into Interest and Profit of Enterprise. Interest-bearing Capital'. However, this also proved to be the least organised part of Marx's notes. As his editor remarked about the editorial task, 'The greatest difficulty was presented by Part V which dealt with the most complicated subject in the entire volume ... Here ... was no finished draft, not even a scheme whose outlines might have been filled out, but only the beginning of an elaboration.'[1]

After three failed attempts to complete Marx's elaboration, Engels restricted himself merely to tidying up Marx's notes. However, the essential start of the section (chapters XXI to XXIV), and chapters XXVII and XXIX were more or less complete. These contain the main elements of Marx's ideas on finance in the capitalist economy. Those ideas may be divided more or less into his theory of interest, and the rest being his theory of money and finance.

Marx regarded modern capitalist finance as having emerged from the finance that was used by capitalist traders from historic times. The latter was the circulating capital that was used to buy stocks of goods in one market for resale in another, often geographically distant market. The payment of interest on the credit required to finance cargoes and their transport then arouses the mercantile reaction against usury, which Marx illustrated with Martin Luther's condemnation of the practice.[2] However, the emergence of industrial capitalism gives rise to what is called today 'financial innovation'. The new capitalism required credit to finance industrial undertakings. The amounts of that credit that are needed are much larger, and the term of the credits (the period of time for which those credits are needed) is much longer.[3] This gives rise to what for Marx is a distinct form of credit, namely 'interest-bearing capital'.

In his analysis of interest-bearing capital Marx was expressly concerned to show that interest is a portion of surplus value, rather than a property of money. Here again he emphasised that monetary appearance needs to be distinguished from the reality of the production and exchanges that give rise to the payment of interest. Because interest appears to be independent of the underlying process of production that generates the surplus value, those who deal in money capital perceive their money capital as generating interest. Later, by the turn of the twentieth century, Veblen would take this distinction further, arguing that the money capital is merely the legal basis of the claim on a part of the surplus that is interest, rather than the source of that interest.[4] But as a materialist Hegelian, Marx was concerned once more to distinguish appearance from a reality rooted in a social process of production and distribution.

Marx therefore returned to his recurrent theme of the centrality of industrial production in determining the nature and dynamics of the capitalist system. 'Vulgar political economy, which seeks to represent capital as an independent source of value' for which the appearance of money capital generating interest, 'is a veritable find, a form in which the source of profit is no longer discernible'. Money capital becomes 'a commodity whose capacity for self-expansion has a definite price quoted every time in the prevailing rate of interest'.[5]

While noting the high rate of interest that obtains in times of crisis, Marx correctly saw this as being a symptom of economic crisis, or the over-extension of credit, rather than as being the cause of crisis, as it appears at the time.[6] In other words, and looking forward to Keynes's contribution to the theory of interest, the higher rate of interest reflects the illiquidity of the borrowers rather than monetary policy or banking considerations on the part of the lenders.[7]

One other remark looks even more strikingly forward to the political economy of Keynes. The latter made the elimination of interest income the key to the socialisation of capital: 'the euthanasia of the rentier, and, consequently, the euthanasia of the cumulative oppressive power of the capitalist to exploit the scarcity-value of capital ... the rentier aspect of capitalism as a transitional phase [which] will disappear when it has done its work ... the euthanasia of the rentier, of the functionless investor'. This was to be achieved by a policy of maintaining low interest rates in order to encourage business investment on such a scale as to obtain full employment.[8]

Marx made much the same kind of claim for the ability of low interest rates to secure high rates of fixed capital investment, but without Keynes's optimism that this will lead to a newer, more benign form of capitalism. Marx did not share Keynes's belief, derived from Marshall, that 'scarcity' is the source of the profit on capital. The development of credit to support industrial capitalism, and the emergence of interest-bearing capital, would give rise to a division among capitalists between 'money capitalists' who lived from the interest, and 'functioning capitalists' who did the actual organisation of industrial production. He considered as 'absurd' the 'idea of converting all the capital into money-capital, without there being people who buy and put to use means of production'. Any attempt to do so would result in 'a frightful depreciation of money-capital and a frightful fall in the rate of interest; many would at once face the impossibility of living on their interest, and would hence be compelled to reconvert into industrial capitalists'.[9] Keynes's analysis not only confused scarcity of money capital, which determines the rate of interest, with scarcity of productive capital. It also postulates the possibility that capitalists can be driven by a low rate of interest to accumulate until capital is no longer 'scarce': a truly utopian vision, since no capitalist would produce or install productive capacity that is so common as to lack a return.

Nevertheless, for Marx, as well as for many of his followers, and many post-Keynesians[10] up to the present day, interest in a capitalist society is impossible without some kind of underlying productive process generating surplus value. This is indeed the case for industrial capitalism, a form of capitalism marked, according to Marx, by 'the subordination of interest-bearing capital to the conditions and requirements of the capitalist mode of production'.[11] But the process of financial innovation evoked by the credit needs of industrial capitalism did not cease with the emergence of interest-bearing capital. After Marx had completed his drafts of Volumes II and III of *Capital*, a series of Companies Acts were passed in Britain and emulated in other capitalist countries. These facilitated the routine establishment of companies. But their more important function was to allow companies that were legally registered to raise long-term finance, in the form of shares or bonds, without the trouble of getting special legislation passed by parliament, as had been the case with railway and canal companies. Those bonds and shares could be traded on the stock market, and there had the advantage, for companies, of assuring long-term finance, while at the same time allowing the suppliers of such finance the possibility of immediate conversion into cash, or liquidity, in the stock market.

2.2   LONG-TERM FINANCE AND CAPITALIST REPRODUCTION

The Companies Acts changed the way in which interest-bearing capital functioned in the capitalist economy. For Marx, the market for interest-bearing capital was like a credit club of 'functioning' and 'money' capitalists, lending each other money to cover the liquidity needs of business, i.e. the need to pay business expenses when current income from sales is insufficient. His remarks on joint stock finance refer merely to the use of this organisational form as a means by which managers defraud shareholders.[12] Marx's editor, Friedrich Engels, was aware that the new stock markets changed the situation, but he understood those changes only superficially. He added to Volume III of *Capital* a brief chapter on the stock exchange bemoaning the spread of the joint stock company form and the swindles and speculation that accompanied it.[13]

However, there was more to the changes wrought by the rise of the business corporation. In the first place, the enhanced ability to raise long-term finance lessened the dependence of industrial capitalists on short-term borrowing. In turn, this changed the character of credit crises. A business that ties up capital in industrial equipment and premises, what Marx called 'constant capital', but finances it with short-term borrowing, needs to 'roll over' (or borrow serially over time to repay the short-term loans) that borrowing over the life-time of the equipment and premises. This makes the business vulnerable to rises in interest rates or a refusal to extend the loan, or an inability to roll over the loans. These were the kinds of illiquidity problems that featured in Marx's account of the financial crises that plagued capitalism.[14]

These problems remain for the stratum of 'functioning' capitalists unable to access the sources of long-term finance in the stock market, usually smaller or medium-sized companies. But for the largest capitalist businesses that can raise such long-term finance, the markets for such finance offer new possibilities. Some of those possibilities, namely the concentration and centralisation of capital, had already been foreseen by Marx. The stock market allows this to take place much more rapidly through mergers and corporate takeovers, when long-term finance is available. However, the markets also offered possibilities for the generation of profits from financial operations that challenge Marx's insistence that there can be no interest without some process of industrial production, i.e. through capital gains in the stock market. It allows 'functioning' capitalists to match more easily the terms of their financial liabilities to their expected cash flow from their business, what Minsky was later to call 'hedge' finance. Here share capital, which does not have to be repaid and on which dividend payments are, in theory at least, discretionary, plays a key role in stabilising the finances of capitalist business.

But the new markets for long-term finance were only the first stage of the financial innovation process. As John Hobson pointed out, the secondary markets in long-term securities issued by capitalists mean that the bonds and shares that those capitalists issue may be used as security for loans, because the market can offer an immediate valuation of these securities. Credit innovation therefore extends the credit available to 'money capitalists' holding such securities.[15] In this way, long-term finance not only insulates 'functioning' capitalists from problems of refinancing. It also extends the liquidity of money capitalists. Moreover, such credit innovation introduces a Wicksellian 'pure credit' system of intermediation in which the balance sheets of the banks intermediate the operations of capitalists. In turn, such a pure credit system facilitates the emergence of Minsky-style balance sheet operations, in which cash flow generated from production is augmented by cash flow from sale of assets and issue of new liabilities.[16]

The key point of Marx's analysis in regard to the new markets in long-term finance is in the effect that those markets have on the turnover of capital. In Volume II of *Capital* Marx had shown that the quantity of surplus obtained by capitalists is influenced by the period of turnover of capital. A shorter period of turnover will, with a given rate of surplus value, generate a higher surplus over a given period of time.[17] In Volume III, Marx reiterated his argument using examples of transport innovations such as railways or the opening of the Suez Canal as cases in which the turnover of capital is reduced.[18] Long-term finance offers new scope for such reductions. This may be illustrated by considering the case of a capitalist who decides to over-capitalise his business, that is, he issues more bond or share capital than is necessary for the purchase of premises or equipment in his business. The capitalist's excess capital is then kept on deposit in the bank, or used to buy bills issued by other capitalists. Our capitalist is now in part a 'functioning' capitalist and, in part, a 'money' capitalist. This much is hinted at by Marx when considering the case of a functioning capitalist operating with just enough capital for his business: 'The employer of capital, even when working with his own capital, splits into two personalities – the owner of capital and the employer of capital; with reference to the categories of profit that it yields, his capital also splits into capital-property, capital outside the production process and yielding interest of itself, and capital in the production process which yields a profit of enterprise through its function.'[19]

However, the excess capital is now turned over in the banking or financial markets with short periods of turnover determined by the terms of the bank deposit or the company bills. The capitalist forgoes the entrepreneurial profit (the difference between the rate of surplus value and the rate of interest) on his excess capital. But his business is now more liquid than it previously was. The entrepreneurial capital forgone may therefore be regarded as a 'cost of liquidity' for the capitalist.[20]

Many of these developments were partially incorporated in the 'finance capital' extensions of Marx's theory by Rudolf Hilferding.[21] Specifically, Hilferding identified a 'monopoly capital' sector organised by and integrated with the new financial markets and obtaining a higher and more stable return on capital than smaller competitive capitalists surviving with only limited support from the credit system. However, Hilferding's view that this would stabilise capitalism and eventually lead to its socialisation was unduly optimistic, even if shared (implicitly) by Keynes. The critical analysis of the effects of long-term finance on capitalism is due more to Rosa Luxemburg, John Maynard Keynes, Michał Kalecki, Josef Steindl, Irving Fisher, Henry Simons, Paul Sweezy, and Hyman Minsky than to Karl Marx or Friedrich Engels.

The development of long-term finance gives a structure of corporate finance or business banking that has important implications for the way in which the capitalist economy functions. The previously mentioned authors carried within his or her analysis of credit an implied balance sheet structure of that corporate finance and how it affected capitalist reproduction.

In the analysis put forward by Marx in Volume III of *Capital* capitalists are 'undercapitalised' in the sense that, as noted above, they have to use short-term borrowing to finance long-term productive assets. The capitalists' banks have balance sheets (excluding trade loans and deposits) that consist of short-term deposits on the liabilities' side, and short-term loans that have been tied up in illiquid productive equipment and premises that have only been partially financed with long-term capital. This is much the same kind of bank balance sheet that Minsky put forward over a century later.[22]

The bank balance sheets that appear in the analysis of Rudolf Hilferding reflect two changes in capitalism since Marx wrote *Capital*. The first is the process of centralisation of capital, resulting in the rise of monopoly capital, and the second the provision to those monopolies of long-term capital. Accordingly, the banking system more or less divides into two: that part of it that serves the monopoly capitalists or the cartelised sector of the economy, and that part which serves capitalists operating in the competitive sector. The first part serving monopoly capitalists corresponds more or less to Hilferding's 'finance capital'. The bank balance sheets of this part have, on their liabilities side, the deposits of the monopoly capitalists and, on their assets side, the banks' long-term loans and bonds and shares issued by the monopoly capitalists. Those balance sheets are kept stable by the monopolists' control over and regulation of markets. The second part of the corporate banks' balance sheets corresponds to the deposits of the competitive capitalists, and bank loans to those capitalists. Since they have no market power, these are the capitalists whose production and sales have to accommodate changes in markets. This makes their finances less stable and, as Hilferding argued, creates an incentive for them to enter the cartelised sector, in which their activity is regulated by the banks and their finances are correspondingly stabilised. The whole process is Hilferding's socialisation of capital by finance. Hilferding also considered the export of capital as a way of assisting in the realisation of surplus. In bank balance sheet terms, this would consist of loans to foreign countries, especially loans to countries subject to imperialist expansion, whose counterpart would be the deposits that finance capitalism gains with the export of capital.

The case that Rosa Luxemburg put forward in *The Accumulation of Capital* is more complex, and offers a less benign outcome to the process of the extension of long-term finance. The implied corporate banking structure similarly has on its liabilities side the deposits of capitalists. But the assets now have, among the loans and bonds issued by capitalist firms, loans to governments for military expenditure and loans to the developing countries for the purpose of creating industrial capacity. Government loans and developing country loans generate deposits for capitalists through their production of the arms that are bought by governments and the industrial equipment shipped to developing countries. But the ability of those governments and the industrialists in developing countries, to pay on their loans is the weakest link in the circuits of this kind of capital and when this breaks, it does so in crisis.

Kalecki used Hilferding's distinction between capitalists in the monopoly sector of the economy, and capitalists operating in competitive markets to show that, far from coming to a stable outcome, the whole system becomes less stable. Kalecki, followed by Josef Steindl, argued that monopolists would be operating with excess capacity and reserves of bank deposits. Excess capacity discourages investment. New loans for investment would therefore be taken out by competitive capitalists. However, their weaker competitive position in their markets would mean that the profits and bank deposits that accrue as a result of their borrowing and investment would be earned by monopoly capitalists. This causes the balance sheets of the corporate banking system to deteriorate in quality because liabilities accrue to monopoly capitalists backed by assets, represented by loans to competitive capitalists who have greater difficulty in servicing their debts.[23]

In the case of Keynes, capitalist enterprise is determined by the rate of interest on long-term bonds, i.e. the terms of long-term financing of capitalists. This relationship between the long-term rate of interest and capital accumulation periodically breaks down due to shifts in capitalists' expectations of future profits. But differences between capitalists in their financing are not really examined, although there is no doubt that Keynes must have been aware of differential access for capitalists to long-term finance. When credit markets freeze up in the face of capitalists' unwillingness to use credit for production, government borrowing is used to circulate credit through the economy.

Minsky followed Keynes in not distinguishing between capitalists with access to long-term finance, and capitalists who do not have that access, and in using government borrowing as a substitute for industrial circulation. Minsky's analysis focuses on the expansion in bank balance sheets over an investment boom. The boom is assumed to be financed in large part by bank borrowing, especially in the later, more speculative part of the boom. Investment in each successive period is therefore presumed to generate successive increases in the debt of capitalists, and this accumulation of debt eventually causes the breakdown of the boom.[24] The contradiction in Minsky's analysis is that he does not really distinguish between the stable, and stabilising, long-term finance available to big capitalist enterprises, and the short-term debt finance to which smaller capitalist firms are confined. Moreover, he fails to identify what happens to the deposit counterpart of the increase in borrowing.[25]

2.3   CONCLUSION

Marx's analysis of interest-bearing capital is the first coherent attempt to integrate finance into a more general theory of capitalist reproduction. Interest-bearing capital comes into being in response to the credit needs of capitalist production. The development of interest-bearing capital into long-term financing for functioning industrial capitalists then divides capitalist enterprises according to their access to long-term finance. This is the foundation of modern corporate finance and its pathologies from the twentieth century.

NOTES

1.   Engels 1970a.
2.   Marx 1959, pp. 610–611.
3.   Niebyl 1946, Chapter 3.
4.   Veblen 1904. See also Marx 1959, p. 355.
5.   Marx 1959, pp. 392–393.
6.   Marx 1959, pp. 406–410.
7.   Marx 1959, p. 361. Marx's theory of interest is further examined in Toporowski 2019.
8.   Keynes 1936, pp. 375–376.
9.   Marx 1959, pp. 377–378.
10. E.g. Hein 2012.
11. Marx 1959, p. 600.
12. 'On the basis of capitalist production a new swindle develops in stock enterprises with respect to the wages of management …', Marx 1959, p. 389.
13. Engels 1970b.
14. Marx 1959, pp. 406–410.
15. 'A constantly increasing proportion of business is conducted by large firms whose capital is expressed in shares negotiable as a basis for bank credit, or whose separate transactions are of a scale and a publicity accommodated to the credit system', Hobson 1913, p. 78.
16. Minsky 1975, pp. 123–127.
17. Marx 1974, pp. 291–295.
18. Marx 1959, p. 71; Marx 1974, pp. 255–256.
19. Marx 1959, p. 375.

20. Toporowski 2008b, pp. 1–10.
21. Hilferding 1910.
22. Minsky 1975, pp. 123–124.
23. Kalecki 1968b; Steindl 1952.
24. Minsky 1986. In this analysis, Minsky was following Irving Fisher's 1933 paper.
25. Lavoie and Seccareccia 2001; Toporowski 2012.

3. Rosa Luxemburg and the Marxists on finance

Rosa Luxemburg is best known for her attempt in her book *The Accumulation of Capital*[1] to show that capitalist accumulation requires external markets in order to overcome a tendency to stagnation. These external markets formed the basis of her theory of imperialism, which was absorbed, often critically, sometimes unwittingly, by Lenin and subsequent Marxists. The English edition of her book, unfortunately, omitted the sub-title of her book, 'Ein Beitrag zur ökonomischen Erklärung des Imperialismus' (A Contribution to an Economic Interpretation of Imperialism). In Chapter 30 of that book, on 'International Loans', Rosa Luxemburg examined the role of finance in capital accumulation. This analysis was perhaps peripheral to her argument. But it has sufficient critical elements to warrant a place for Luxemburg among the pioneers of critical finance, while the fate of that analysis among Marxists reveals how the most important school of radical political economy in the twentieth century came to an attenuated view of finance as a factor in capitalist crisis. In this chapter, it is argued that Luxemburg put forward an analysis of international finance that not only captures a disturbing character of finance, but also looks forward to important aspects of Minsky's analysis in the second half of the twentieth century.

3.1 ROSA LUXEMBURG'S CRITICISM OF INTERNATIONAL BANKING

For Luxemburg, the context of the system of international loans was crucial. Advanced capitalist countries faced crises of 'realisation', i.e. inadequate demand to allow profits to accrue. This was the basis of her argument with other Marxists, who argued that exploitation of workers' labour – making them work for longer than was necessary to produce the equivalent of their wages – is sufficient to generate a profit.[2] For Luxemburg, the additional labour was useless to capitalists unless it could be sold, and in this way converted into money: Capitalists are interested in profits in the form of money, and not in the form of surplus products. At the same time, developing countries lacked the markets for commodity production to take place on a capitalist scale, or to absorb the surplus production of developed capitalist countries. She argued that international loans are crucial in providing finance so that dependent and colonial countries can buy the equipment to develop their economic and industrial infrastructure, reaching political independence but tied into financial dependence on the older capitalist states:

> In the Imperialist Era, the foreign loan played an outstanding part as a means for young capitalist countries to acquire independence. The contradictions inherent in the modern system of foreign loans are the concrete expression of those which characterise the imperialist phase. Though foreign loans are indispensable for the emancipation of the rising capitalist states, they are yet the surest ties by which the old capitalist states maintain their influence, exercise financial control and exert pressure on the customs, foreign and commercial policy of the young capitalist states ... such loans widen the scope for the accumulation of capital; but at the same time they restrict it by creating new competition for the investing countries.[3]

The raising of loans and the sale of bonds therefore occur in exaggerated anticipation of profits. When those hopes are dashed, a crisis of over-indebtedness breaks out. The governments of the dependent and colonial territories are obliged to socialise the debts, and make them a charge on their tax revenues. However, by this time the loans have served their primary purpose, which is to finance the export of capital equipment from the advanced capitalist countries, thereby adding to their profits and capital accumulation. With the crisis, capital accumulation comes to a halt, before new issues of bonds and loans finance capital exports to another country and capital accumulation is resumed.

The financial crisis is overcome mainly at the cost of destroying the agricultural economy of the developing countries:

> While the realisation of the surplus value requires only the general spreading of commodity production, its capitalisation demands the progressive supercession of simple commodity production by capitalist economy, with the corollary that the limits to both the realisation and the capitalisation of surplus value keep contracting ever more.[4]

Ultimately the peasants have to pay the additional taxes and are destined to see their markets taken over by mass capitalist production. Luxemburg gave an extensive account of international loans in Egypt as an example. Here:

> The transactions between European loan capital and industrial capital are based upon relations which are extremely rational and 'sound' for the accumulation of capital, because this loan capital pays for the orders from Egypt and the interest on one loan is paid out of a new loan. Stripped of all obscuring connecting links, these relations consist in the simple fact that European capital has largely swallowed up the Egyptian peasant economy. Enormous tracts of land, labour and labour products, accruing to the state as taxes, have ultimately been converted into European capital and have been accumulated ... As against the fantastic increase of capital on the one hand, the other economic result is the ruin of peasant economy together with the growth of commodity exchange ...[5]

Similarly, in Turkey, 'railroad building and commodity exchange ... are fostered by the state on the basis of the rapid disintegration, ruin and exploitation of Asiatic peasant economy in the course of which the Turkish state becomes more and more dependent on European capital, politically as well as financially'.[6]

3.2   THE MARXIAN REFLECTIVE VIEW OF FINANCE

Luxemburg's analysis of finance did not win the favour of contemporary Marxist economists, who remained largely wedded to a view that financial developments must be a reflection of 'contradictions' arising in the processes of production that finance was supposed to fund. This was despite occasional hints that maybe finance was becoming an autonomous factor in capitalist development. In his pamphlet, *Imperialism, the Highest Stage of Capitalism*,[7] written in 1917, Lenin did not even mention Rosa Luxemburg, but based his economic explanation of imperialism on his critical reading of Hobson's *Imperialism*, and his view of the role of finance in Hilferding's *Finance Capital*. Hilferding's book had been published in 1910, three years before Luxemburg's, and put forward a more benign view of finance. Hilferding generalised from the experience of banking in Germany, where 'universal' banks organised the capital markets and thereby came to own often controlling stakes in large companies. He argued that banks were a crucial factor in the emergence of monopoly capitalism and the cartelisation of the capitalist economy. In Hilferding's view, the banks not only financed the industrial expansion of capitalism into dependent and colonial territories, but also restrained competition between capitalists and financed their cartels. If crises arose, they were due to disproportions in production and class struggles. By stabilising the markets and finances of the capitalists in their cartels, banks were able to shift the costs of those crises onto non-cartelised capitalists. Because it concentrates control over industry, finance capital facilitates the eventual socialisation of the means of production.[8]

In his insistence that capitalist crisis can only be due to disproportions in production, or struggles between the classes involved in it, Hilferding was undoubtedly the more orthodox Marxist. Marx's views on money and finance do not constitute a consistent analysis, largely because in his time finance was only just emerging into economic pre-eminence. Recent research by Anitra Nelson and Riccardo Bellofiore suggests those views themselves appear to have been mangled in the course of Engels' editing of Marx's notes into the widely accepted versions of the second and third volumes of *Capital*.[9] However, in at least two respects Marx was in advance of the conventional, Ricardian thinking of his time. First of all, Marx distinguished explicitly between the rate of interest and the rate of profit: In the classical political economy of David Ricardo, and even later in the work of Eugen Böhm-Bawerk, the rate of interest and the rate of profit were virtually interchangeable.

Second, and related to his distinction between the rate of interest and the rate of profit, Marx distinguished between real, or productive, capital, and the 'fictitious' capital of financial assets.[10] Real capital is the stock of plant, equipment and materials out of which goods will be produced. Fictitious capital is the structure of financial claims on that capital. This is crucial for the process of equalising the rate of profit across industries. It is through the market for fictitious capital that money capital may be advanced to particular industries, and through that market, money may be taken out of particular industries and firms and transferred to others.

The scope and significance of finance in Marx's analysis is clearly laid out in Chapter XXXVI of Volume III of *Capital*. With the title 'Pre-capitalist Relations' it may seem an odd chapter in which to find Marx's conclusions on the role of finance in capitalism. But it does conclude Part V of the volume, a part that is entitled 'Division of Profit into Interest and Profit of Enterprise. Interest-Bearing Capital'. Moreover, the chapter has the added merit of authenticity: In his Preface, Engels wrote that 'The greatest difficulty was presented by Part V which dealt with the most complicated subject in the entire volume.' After fruitless attempts to complete various chapters in it, Engels confined himself to 'as orderly an arrangement of available matter as possible'. Of these chapters, the manuscript of 'the "Pre-capitalist" chapter (Chapter XXXVI) was quite complete'.[11]

The chapter discusses the historic emergence of credit from medieval systems of usury. Marx wrote that:

> The credit system develops as a reaction against usury. But this should not be misunderstood, nor by any means interpreted in the manner of the ancient writers, the church fathers, Luther or the early socialists. It signifies no more and no less than the subordination of interest-bearing capital to the conditions and requirements of the capitalist mode of production.[12]

Marx viewed the battle against usury as a 'demand for the subordination of interest-bearing capital to industrial capital'.[13]

In this way, capital ceases to be the fragmentary wealth that is at the unhindered disposal of individual capitalists, but is socialised to be real-located where the highest return may be obtained.

What is crucial here is the use of the word 'subordination'. It clearly indicates the view that finance and credit are led by developments in productive industry.[14] As Engels succinctly put it in a letter to Eduard Bernstein in 1883, 'The stock exchange simply adjusts the *distribution* of the surplus value *already stolen* from the workers ...'.[15] In Volume III of *Capital* such adjustment is supposed to facilitate convergence, among firms and different activities, on an *average* rate of profit, whose decline then sets off *generalised* industrial crisis in capitalism.[16]

Although this could not have been foreseen at the time when Marx was writing, the development of the capitalist system went not towards the 'subordination' of finance to industrial capital, but in fact towards the subordination of industrial capital to finance. Hence the sluggish development of industry in capitalist countries that have come to be dominated by rentier capitalism, most notably the United Kingdom and the United States from the 1880s through to the 1930s, and from the 1980s onwards.

This development is central to the theory of capitalist crisis. In Marx economic depressions are supposed to arise from a decline in the *industrial* rate of profit. Marx, however, recognised that excessive expansion of credit may also give rise to crisis, when confidence in that credit falls, and demand for cash settlements rises. In Volume III of *Capital*, he suggested two kinds of such crisis. One was an internal banking crisis, 'when credit collapses completely and when not only commodities and securities are undiscountable and nothing counts any more but money payment

... Ignorant and mistaken bank legislation, such as that of 1844–1845 can intensify this money crisis. But no kind of bank legislation can eliminate a crisis.'[17]

The other kind of crisis that was familiar to Marx was the drain of gold for international payments attendant upon a balance of payments deficit. This results in the successive ruin of first importers and then exporters: 'over-imports and over-exports have taken place in all countries (we are not speaking here about crop failures etc., but about a general crisis); that is over-production promoted by credit and the general inflation of prices that goes with it'.[18] However, more modern crises of finance capitalism appear to be set off by disturbances in the financial system, which then spread to industry by devastating the balance sheets of industrial corporations. Notable examples of this are the 1929 Crash and the Japanese economic crisis after 1991. For Marxists these raise very fundamental questions concerning the scope of Marx's analysis, that is, the degree to which it indicates salient features of the capitalism of his time, and the degree to which that analysis remains true of capitalism everywhere at all times. This is not a dilemma peculiar to Marxists. It is one that affects adherents of all 'defunct economists'. Perhaps most of all it affects those 'practical men who believe themselves to be quite exempt from any intellectual influences' and who therefore do not yet understand that their 'obvious' ideas were invented by some defunct economist to enlighten circumstances that have since passed away.

Marx made one further assumption that today would be considered controversial. This concerns the manner in which capitalist finance operates. One paragraph below his statement that capitalist finance is subordinated to industry, Marx wrote the following:

> What distinguishes interest-bearing capital – in so far as it is an essential element of the capitalist mode of production – from usurer's capital is by no means the nature and character of this capital itself. It is merely the altered conditions under which it operates, and consequently also the totally transformed character of the borrower, who confronts the money-lender. Even when a man without fortune receives credit in his capacity of industrialist or merchant, it occurs with the expectation that he will function as a capitalist and appropriate unpaid labour with the borrowed capital. He receives credit in his capacity of potential capitalist. The circumstance that a man without fortune but possessing energy, solidity, ability and business acumen may become a capitalist in this manner – and the commercial value of each individual is pretty accurately estimated under the capitalist mode of production – is greatly admired by apologists of the capitalist system. Although this circumstance continually brings an unwelcome number of new soldiers of

fortune into the field and into competition with the already existing individual capitalists, it also reinforces the supremacy of capital itself, expands its base and enables it to recruit ever new forces for itself out of the substratum of society. In a similar way, the circumstance that the Catholic Church in the Middle Ages formed its hierarchy out of the best brains in the land, regardless of their estate, birth or fortune, was one of the principal means of consolidating ecclesiastical rule and suppressing the laity. The more a ruling class is able to assimilate the foremost minds of a ruled class, the more stable and dangerous becomes its rule.[19]

This Schumpeterian vision comes close to the perfectly efficient intermediation view of finance. It is still the view that prevails in contemporary economics. The more fundamental critic of capitalism, in this regard, turns out to have been Michał Kalecki, who concluded that the key factor in capital accumulation was the 'free' capital owned by the entrepreneur. He wrote that:

The limitation of the size of the firm by the availability of entrepreneurial capital goes to the very heart of the capitalist system. Many economists assume, at least in their abstract theories, a state of business democracy where anybody endowed with entrepreneurial ability can obtain capital for a business venture. This picture of the activities of the 'pure' entrepreneur is, to put it mildly, unrealistic. The most important prerequisite for becoming an entrepreneur is the *ownership* of capital.[20]

Hints at a more complex view of finance by the founders of the Marxist school emerge in their correspondence, in particular the later letters which show a lively sensitivity to the way in which finance acquired economic importance as the nineteenth century progressed. In a letter in 1881 to the Russian economist and translator of *Capital* Nikolai Danielson, Marx noted how an influx of gold reserves can insulate the financial system from the industrial crisis: '... if the great industrial and commercial crisis England has passed through went over without the culminating financial crash at London, this *exceptional* phenomenon was only due to French money'.[21] In a later letter to the German social democrat leader August Bebel, in 1885, Engels noted how inflated financial markets would drive down interest rates. In the absence of higher returns from industry, money markets would stay liquid, but their liquidity would

not induce industrial investment, a premonition of later English theories
of liquidity preference:

> The chronic depression in all the decisive branches of industry also still con-
> tinues unbroken here, in France and in America. Especially in iron and cotton.
> It is an unheard-of situation, though entirely the inevitable result of the cap-
> italist system: such colossal over-production that it cannot even bring things
> to a crisis! The over-production of disposable capital seeking investment is so
> great that the rate of discount here actually fluctuates between 1 and 1½ per
> cent per annum, and for money invested in short-term credits, which can be
> called in or paid off from day to day (money on call) one can hardly get ½ per
> cent per annum. But by choosing to invest his money in this way than in new
> industrial undertakings the money capitalist is admitting how rotten the whole
> business looks to him. And this fear of new investments and old enterprises,
> which had already manifested itself in the crisis of 1867, is the main reason
> why things are not brought to an acute crisis.[22]

Finally, in 1890, looking back on his early years as an industrialist,
Engels bemoaned the distorted view of industry that prevails in the financial markets and their self-regarding nature. He admitted that financial
crises may occur that have little or no foundation in industrial reverses.
Finance may develop in its own way, but is an arena for the struggle
between various industrial interests. But ultimately the financial system
must reflect production 'taken as a whole'. Engels' letter to the Swiss
journalist Conrad Schmidt, date 27 October 1890, stands out as a succinct
statement of the Marxian 'reflective' view of finance:

> The money market man only sees the movement of industry and of the world
> market in the inverted reflection of the money and the stock market and so
> effect becomes cause to him. I noted that in the 'forties already in Manchester:
> the London Stock Exchange reports were utterly useless for the course of
> industry and its periodical maxima and minima because these gentry tried to
> explain everything from crises on the money markets which were generally
> only symptoms. At that time, the object was to explain away the origin of
> industrial crises as temporary over-production, so that the thing had in addi-
> tion its tendentious side, provocative of distortion. This point has not gone
> (for us, at any rate, for good and all), added to which it is indeed a fact that
> the money market can also have its own crises, in which direct disturbances
> of industry only play a subordinate part or no part at all – here there is still
> much, especially in the history of the last twenty years, to be examined and
> established …
> As soon as trading in money becomes separate from trade in commodities it
> has (under certain conditions imposed by production and commodity trade
> and within these limits) a development of its own, special laws and special
> phases determined by its own nature. If, in this further development, trade

in money extends in addition to trade in securities and these securities are not only government securities but also industrial and transport stocks and shares, so that money trade conquers the direct control over a portion of the production by which, taken as a whole, it is itself controlled, then the reaction of money trading on production becomes still stronger and more complicated. The money traders have become the owners of railways, mines, iron works, etc. These means of production take on a double aspect: their working has to be directed sometimes in the immediate interests of production, but sometimes also according to the requirements of the shareholders, in so far as they are money traders. The most striking example of this is the American railways, whose working is entirely dependent on the stock exchange operations of a Jay Gould or a Vanderbilt, etc., these have nothing whatever to do with the particular railway concerned and its interests as a means of communication. And even here in England we have seen struggles lasting for tens of years between different railway companies over the boundaries of their respective territories – struggles in which an enormous amount of money was thrown away, not in the interests of production and communications, but simply because of a rivalry which usually only had the object of facilitating the stock exchange dealings of the shareholding money traders.[23]

In his critique of Luxemburg, Lenin's associate Nikolai Bukharin rebuked her for exaggerating the need for external markets and her neglect of finance as a centralising element in monopoly capitalism.[24] In line with Hilferding's analysis of finance as coordinating monopoly capitalism, Marxist critics have largely followed the founders of their school of thought to adhere to a 'reflective' view that, if financial crisis occurs, it is because it correctly 'reflects' critical developments in production: a fall in the rate of profit, increased class struggle, disproportions, and so on. Even after the 1929 Crash, the Hungarian-Soviet economist Eugene Varga provided a Marxist orthodoxy according to which 'the cause of the cyclical course of capitalist production is the accumulation of capital' resulting in excess industrial capacity.[25] The collapse of the long-term capital market was caused by such excess capacity.[26] More recently, Suzanne de Brunhoff went as far as any Marxist critic has gone in writing that: '...the financial cycle is only a reflection of the economic cycle: monetary and financial movements reflect non-monetary and non-financial internal and international disturbances. But they reflect them *in their own way* because of the existence of specific financial structures.'[27] However, 'the capitalist form of production is unable to give an entirely functional character to the conditions under which it functions; the credit system preserves a relatively autonomous development. The resurgence of the monetary system in times of crisis is a sign of that autonomy, since the demand for money is completely outside the movement of real production. But the financial crisis also reduces the "fictitious" mushrooming of credits and restores the monetary basis of credit.'[28] But this is because stock prices and credit can fluctuate with a degree of independence of real capital, and inversely with the rate of interest.[29]

3.3   LUXEMBURG, FINANCE AND MINSKY

There is another aspect of Luxemburg's approach to finance that looks forward to the analysis of Hyman P. Minsky in the second half of the twentieth century. Minsky is well known as the author of the 'financial instability hypothesis' in which the progress of capitalist prosperity or growth autonomously generates circumstances of financial 'fragility' and crisis. Minsky, like many US authors, had in the forefront of his mind the economic debilitation that was caused in his country by the 1929 Crash. He favoured government intervention to stabilise aggregate demand, as well as central bank loosening of monetary policy, to keep financial crisis at bay.[30] His political economy of finance was essentially a Keynesian one in which the state takes an active role in stabilising the financial system of its country.

Rosa Luxemburg's political economy of finance is somewhat different, but arguably is no less current than Minsky's. In her analysis, the financial system is international, but based in the advanced capitalist countries (as it is today). Governments are weak and, in the poorer countries, are dependent upon the international financial system for financing their loans. By contrast, Minsky's analysis had in mind the US government, and governments of advanced capitalist countries that are less dependent upon the international financial system, or at least have greater scope for manipulating it than is available to governments of poorer countries.

A much more distinctive feature of Luxemburg's political economy of finance, by comparison with Minsky's, lies in the way in which financial risk is socialised and the consequences of that socialisation. Minsky envisaged that a socialisation of financial risk would allow domestic business to flourish, with its markets underpinned jointly by financial stability and a welfare state. Luxemburg recognised that, in poorer countries, the socialisation of financial risk, through state guarantees of commercial foreign debts, has costs that are unequally distributed between locally based and foreign-based enterprises. The locally based ones, largely in traditional activities, have virtually no possibilities to escape from the tax demands of their government. Foreign-based enterprises,

usually in the more modern sector of the economy, have huge possibilities of escape. Hence, the costs of foreign indebtedness in less developed
countries are borne by the traditional sector that benefits least from
foreign investment. Over the longer term, the traditional sector becomes
economically marginalised, and the traditional state that underwrites the
country's foreign debts becomes politically marginalised. In this way the
developing world approaches the neo-liberal ideal of a small state, whose
apparent partiality for business masks an oppressive concentration of tax
and debt burdens on households and businesses in the traditional sector.
The economic dynamics of such states are then determined by financial
inflows of foreign aid, and the pulse of foreign direct investment, punctu-
ated by natural disasters and civil disorders.

The socialisation of risk in the more advanced capitalist countries
envisaged by Minsky has somewhat different consequences. The sharing
of the risks of financial enterprise facilitates credit inflation in capital
markets in particular. The result has been apparent in recent years, in the
United States and in Europe, in growing industrial concentration, and the
rising influence of financial institutions over industrial corporations. But
far from facilitating continuing accumulation, as Hilferding and to some
degree Minsky expected, the combination of the socialisation of financial
risk and industrial concentration has led, in the United States and the
United Kingdom at least, to industrial stagnation, or slow growth at best.
The 'monopoly capital' school of Marxist analysis had no doubt that this
industrial stagnation was due to the decline of industrial competition.
But a case may also be made for a more Veblenian analysis in which, as
a result of financial market stabilisation, companies find that profits from
refinancing their operations in the financial markets may be more easily
and cleanly obtained than from productive activities. This was a possibility that Minsky foresaw, but to which he advanced no remedy.

3.4   CONCLUSION

Karl Polanyi, in his pioneering study of the social and institutional roots
of economic and financial collapse in the 1930s, wrote that 'Marxist
works, like Hilferding's or Lenin's studies, stressed the imperialistic
forces emanating from national banking, and their organic connection
with the heavy industries. Such an argument, besides being restricted
mainly to Germany, necessarily failed to deal with international banking
interests.'[31] In this regard Rosa Luxemburg was exceptional. Her analysis
of the international loans system in the period preceding the First World

War may have been incidental to her main argument about capitalist accumulation. But the view she portrayed of a financial system that visits repeated catastrophes on the traditional economy, in the course of incorporating it in the modern international capitalist economy, anticipates much of the experience of developing countries since the 1970s. The elements of critical finance in her work survive better than the model of accumulation in which they were framed.

NOTES

1. Luxemburg 1951.
2. This controversy is extensively reviewed by Tadeusz Kowalik in his masterly book *Rosa Luxemburg: Theory of Accumulation and Imperialism* (Kowalik 2014).
3. Luxemburg 1951, p. 421.
4. Ibid.
5. Ibid., p. 438; see also Aaronovitch 1946.
6. Luxemburg 1951, p. 445.
7. Lenin 1917.
8. Hilferding 1910, chapters 20 and 25.
9. Nelson 1998; see also Bellofiore 1998.
10. Marx 1959, Chapter XXV.
11. Ibid., pp. 4 and 6.
12. Ibid., p. 600.
13. Ibid., p. 603.
14. As in nearly everything that Marx wrote after the first volume of *Capital*, it is possible to question the interpretation of his analysis, because of the enormous scope that his notes left for editing. But this chapter suffered least from Engels' editing, and it has not been mis-translated: In the original German, the sentence about the subordination of finance to industrial production reads as follows: 'Es bedeutet nichts mehr und nichts weniger al die Unterordnung des zinstragenden Kapitals unter den Bedingungen und Bedürfnisse der kapitalistischen Produktionweise' (Marx 1932, pp. 647–648). Suzanne de Brunhoff prefers to use the word 'adapt' in place of 'subordinate' (de Brunhoff 1976, p. 77).
15. Marx and Engels 1992, p. 433.
16. Marx 1959, Parts II and III. An essential guide to the interpretation of these parts was given by Josef Steindl in 'Karl Marx and the Accumulation of Capital' in Steindl 1952.
17. Marx 1959, pp. 459 and 49.
18. Ibid., pp. 491–492. See also Clarke 1994.
19. Marx 1959, pp. 600–601.
20. Kalecki 1954, pp. 94–95. Kalecki went on to commend Steindl's treatment of this problem in the latter's 'Capital Enterprise and Risk' (Steindl 1945a).
21. Marx and Engels 1936, p. 384.
22. Ibid., p. 441.

23. Ibid., pp. 478–480.
24. Bukharin 1924, pp. 253 and 257.
25. Varga 1935, p. 21.
26. Ibid., pp. 39–47.
27. de Brunhoff 1976, pp. 100–101, emphasis in the original.
28. Ibid., p. 118.
29. Marx 1959, pp. 467–469.
30. Minsky 1986.
31. Polanyi 1945, p. 283.

PART II

Critical theories of finance in the twentieth century: unstable money and finance

4. Ralph Hawtrey and the monetary business cycle

If thoughtful individuals, well read in contemporary economic theory in the 1920s, had been asked at that time which economist was most likely to revolutionise twentieth-century monetary economics (and indeed had already started doing so), it is likely that, without hesitation, they would have given the name Ralph Hawtrey, rather than that of his rival, which we would now give, John Maynard Keynes. J.C. Gilbert recalled studying monetary theory from Hawtrey's *Currency and Credit* at the London School of Economics in the 1920s, and Hicks was told by Austin Robinson that this was the standard work used in the Cambridge Tripos at that time.[1] Forty years later, his standing had been reduced to that of one of the 'also-rans' of monetary theory.[2] For example in Roll's standard textbook *A History of Economic Thought*, he merits only one mention as a theorist of credit policy.[3] Schumpeter remarked that 'Throughout the twenties, Hawtrey's theory enjoyed a considerable vogue. In the United States, especially, it was the outstanding rationalization of the uncritical belief in the unlimited efficacy of the open-market operations of the Federal Reserve System that prevailed then.'[4] But this was largely because Hawtrey's ideas were taken up by Allyn Young at Harvard University, who was an occasional adviser to Benjamin Strong, the influential Governor of the Federal Reserve Bank of New York from 1922 to his untimely death in 1928. As late as 1947, Lawrence Klein referred to Hawtrey as Keynes's 'rival for the leadership of British monetary policy'.[5] But Charles Goodhart's scholarly study of *The Evolution of Central Banks* does not even mention Hawtrey.

Much of the obscurity into which his work has fallen is the outcome of the notoriety that became attached to his name because of his authorship and his prolific and sophisticated advocacy in the Great Depression of the 1930s of what was known as the 'Treasury View'. This opposed fiscal stimulus, because it would 'crowd out' private sector investment, and urged 'prompt and large cuts in wages' and, less notoriously, devaluation and credit expansion, as policies for economic revival.[6] Hawtrey's fiscal pessimism and regressive distributional values contrasted inevitably with Keynes's more optimistic view. In the progressive Keynesian consensus that followed 1945, even serious scholars have been inclined to dismiss Hawtrey's work. This is despite the methodological sophistication of his disequilibrium analysis of banking and finance which, unlike that of Keynes, does not obscure that disequilibrium by presenting it in equilibrium terms.[7]

Patrick Deutscher has recently suggested a number of reasons why Hawtrey's analysis fell into disuse. His emphasis on stock-holders' responses to interest rate changes seemed relevant to an earlier, mercantile capitalism, rather than an industrial capitalism based on fixed capital investment. But his earlier work does contain a theory of fixed capital investment. Deutscher says that his ideas were disadvantaged by his absence from an academic milieu. But other, later, contemporaries, such as Michał Kalecki and Paul Sweezy, also worked outside an academic milieu and did not suffer obscurity as a result. Third, Deutscher argues, because Hawtrey was widely perceived to have lost the policy argument of the 1930s, it was assumed that 'the facts falsified his theories'. This was indeed a serious disadvantage for Hawtrey. But it was to some degree remedied when the monetarist counter-revolution brought some of his ideas back into favour, albeit now with superficially Keynesian elements of expectations, rather than stock-holding, as the crucial monetary transmission mechanism. Fourth, Hawtrey's 'aversion to formalism prevented him from working fully within the framework of mainstream economics and obscured his theoretical contributions'.[8] But this is precisely what made him such a popular author in the 1920s. This aversion certainly did not diminish the authority of economists such as Joseph Schumpeter and Gunnar Myrdal, and even added a certain bohemian notoriety to the reputation of John Kenneth Galbraith. Finally, Deutscher argues that Hawtrey was 'dated and made obsolete' by the Keynesian revolution.[9] Much the same could be said of David Ricardo and Keynes's teacher Alfred Marshall, and many students today are taught little more than Ricardo and Marshall in their economics courses. His reputation indeed never recovered from the exposure of his regressive economic values, through his association with the 'Treasury View' that is supposed to have shaped the 'hungry thirties'. Moreover, as macroeconomics developed, his approach in which everything hung on the short-term rate of interest, proved to be methodologically untenable. It was Hawtrey's misfortune that the monetary transmission mechanism from short-term interest rates has become such conventional wisdom in contemporary economics that his immense contribution to establishing this transmission mechanism as the key relationship in economic dynamics is overlooked today.

In the final analysis, it was the inability of his ideas to make the transition from the inter-war ruins of the era of finance that flourished, in the unstable kind of way that he perceived, before the First World War. In the era of planned public sector stabilisation of economic disturbances, after the Second World War, there could be little relevance in a monetary theory of the business cycle. But his most serious failure as an economist was also that aspect of his work which was his greatest achievement from the point of view of this study in critical finance. His underlying economic philosophy that money and finance, left to themselves, will disturb the capitalist economy, remains worthy of re-examination in our present era of finance.

4.1   UNSTABLE MONEY

Hawtrey himself was not discouraged by the success of his younger contemporary, and the apparent anachronism of his own analysis. Towards the end of a life that spanned the final decades of the gold standard, and the beginnings of the emergence of finance at the end of the twentieth century, he reiterated his view as follows:

> To unstable money are to be traced nearly all our economic troubles since 1918: the unemployment of the inter-war period; the over-employment and scarcity of labour since the Second World War; the labour unrest incidental to perpetual wage demands; the hardships and dislocation caused by the declining value of small savings, annuities and endowments; the vexation of continual price rises even for those whose incomes on the whole keep pace with them; the collapse of the prices of Government securities through distrust of the unit in which they are valued.[10]

By 'unstable money', Hawtrey meant considerably more than instability of the purchasing power of money, due to fluctuations in prices. 'Unstable money' meant for him a complex way in which monetary and financial institutions destabilise the economy in which they operate. However, monetary theory was the starting point of Hawtrey's analysis, and it is for his monetary theory of the business cycle that he was best known in his time. Hawtrey's theory is different in a very fundamental way from other monetary business cycle theories. In the monetary business cycle theories of Hayek, and, in the latter part of the century, Friedman, Lucas and, most recently, Wojnilower, monetary disturbances in economic

activity are induced by incorrect economic or, more strictly, monetary
policy decisions. For Hayek and Friedman, the economy is disturbed
when the authorities expand credit by more or less than the amount
required to finance the level of investment and economic activity desired
by the private sector.[11] For Lucas, unexpected changes in the money
supply disturb economic equilibrium.[12] In Wojnilower's analysis, 'credit
crunches', or withdrawals of loan facilities in response to the authorities' reregulation and monetary tightening, cause financial crises.[13] The
starting point, whether explicit or implied, is that in a 'natural' economy,
i.e. without intervention by the authorities, the economy would proceed
without financial crisis.

Hawtrey's starting point was different. He recognised that the institutional forms through which the capitalist system evolved have been
conditions in which money and finance disturb the economy. The roots
of his analysis were in his historical studies of monetary and financial
arrangements and, in particular, the efforts of central banks to ease the
constraints of the gold standard on the credit system in the century before
the First World War, and the attempts to resurrect that standard after that
war. This is epitomised in the content and title of the last book that he
prepared for publication in 1962, a third edition of *A Century of Bank
Rate*. The central banks' interest in more flexible currency policy arose
out of a necessity to avoid the financial crises that the 'cross of gold'
periodically inflicted upon the economy because of changes in the global
supply of gold, and shifts in its distribution among trading countries.
For Hawtrey therefore, the monetary and financial system disturbs the
economy naturally, and requires appropriate economic policies to limit
the resulting instability. Of the authors cited in the previous paragraph,
only Friedman, perhaps and certainly not consciously, with his idea
of a constitutionally ordained rate of monetary expansion to stabilise
the economy, comes anywhere near to Hawtrey's critical approach to
finance.[14]

Hawtrey was largely self-taught in economics. So it is unlikely that the
Swedish originator of credit cycles, Knut Wicksell, influenced Hawtrey,
although both reflected in their respective analyses a more general sense
that money markets do not 'naturally' complement a general economic
equilibrium.[15] Wicksell postulated a 'natural' rate of interest that keeps
the economy in equilibrium by equalising saving with the demand for it
for investment purposes. However, in a money economy, the actual or
money rate of interest is determined in the money markets by the demand
for and supply of money by banks. Since this is subject to change accord-

ing to the cash position of banks, the actual rate of interest differs from the natural rate. If the market rate of interest is above the 'natural' rate, 'forced' saving causes prices and production to fall until equilibrium is reached between the two rates of interest. If the market rate of interest is below the 'natural' rate, saving is too low and prices and production rise until again equilibrium is restored with stable prices and production and equality between the two rates of interest.[16] The centrality of the notion of equilibrium in Wicksell's work is confirmed, and criticised, by Gunnar Myrdal in his *Monetary Equilibrium*, Chapter III. Myrdal and his Swedish contemporaries, Erik Lindahl and Erik Lundberg, developed the elements of a monetary business cycle, based on a Wicksellian cumulative disequilibrium process. However, they stopped short at showing that non-equilibrium interest rates change prices and the level of economic activity. Hawtrey went further and showed how banks can systematically generate and propagate disequilibrium in the economy. Similarly, Irving Fisher had published a theory of a credit cycle, which was brought to the attention of Hawtrey, probably by Keynes, before the writing of *Good and Bad Trade*. But this too, as Keynes was to point out, failed to show systematic generation of economic disturbances.[17] Alfred Marshall, the doyen of English economists at the end of the nineteenth century, had put forward a credit cycle as early as his first excursion into systematic economics with his wife, Mary Paley Marshall, in *The Economics of Industry*. In this, rising prosperity stimulates an expansion of credit which raises prices until speculation is stopped.[18]

But Marshall too was likely to have been only an indirect influence on Hawtrey. He had not taught Hawtrey at Cambridge, where the latter had studied mathematics and had picked up a basic economics education from Sir John Clapham, a distinguished economic historian who also wrote prolifically on banking and financial history. It is perhaps this early influence that is apparent in Hawtrey's inclination throughout his work to explain by reference to the working of markets and institutions rather than to some immanent intellectually derived equilibrium.[19] His analysis bears more than a passing resemblance to the criticisms of the Birmingham Currency School in the first half of the nineteenth century, in particular Thomas Attwood, who criticised (albeit unsystematically) the instability of the gold standard, and questioned the wisdom of allowing 'the pressure of the metallic standard to fall upon the poor' as well as 'the industrious, the useful and the valuable classes of the community'.[20]

In his first book, *Good and Bad Trade*, published in 1913, Hawtrey examined a credit cycle mechanism, but without any equilibrium being

brought about by the markets. Capital investment by traders and entrepreneurs is undertaken in expectation of a rate of profit which he defines
in labour value terms. If this rate of profit is greater than the market rate
of interest, then entrepreneurs will invest and expand production. But if
it is less, then investment and production will be reduced. Investment
and production decisions involve commitments for longer periods of
time, during which currency is drawn out of banks and into the cash
economy in which the majority of the population in Hawtrey's time still
existed. During a boom, therefore, companies find themselves drawing
down their balances in banks. To stem the drain of cash, banks raise their
interest rates. Because these take time to influence current investment
and production, banks find themselves raising interest rates by successive
amounts until investment and production are brought down to levels
that will conserve, and even increase the cash in bank tills. At this point
interest rates are too high, and depression sets in until falling interest
rates have their (delayed) effect on output and trade. In any case, in
contrast to Wicksell's analysis, no equilibrium is ever reached: '... there
is an inherent tendency towards fluctuations in the banking institutions
which prevail in the world as it is'.[21] Hawtrey later criticised the Quantity
Theory of Money over its presumption of stability:

> The banks, by restricting credit, can start the vicious circle of deflation, or, by
> relaxing credit, can start the vicious circle of inflation. Either process, once
> started, tends to continue by its own momentum. In the one case there will
> ensue a cumulative shrinkage of demand, curtailment of output and decline
> of prices; in the other a cumulative expansion of demand, increase of output
> and rise of prices.

Credit is thus *inherently unstable*.[22]

> In practice it seldom, perhaps never, happens that a state of equilibrium is
> actually reached. A period of expanding or contracting credit, when it comes
> to an end, leaves behind it a legacy of adjustments, and before these are half
> completed a new movement has probably already set in.[23]

Hawtrey's distinctive innovation was to lay out this, already in his time,
established explanation of investment on the basis of a theory of credit
and interest rates, and a theory of trade that are very modern, in the sense
of explaining investment and trade in the sophisticated mechanisms of
a finance-dominated economy, rather than in reduction to the elements of
a 'natural' economy. In *Good and Bad Trade*, he compared the functioning of an 'island' economy without money with economies using money,

and then credit. He used this not to establish 'natural laws' or relation-
ships, but to show that a credit economy will not converge on a stable
equilibrium, but will continue to be disturbed by the changing liquidity
of the banking system (Chapter VI of *Good and Bad Trade* is entitled
'A Monetary Disturbance in an Isolated Community with a Banking
System'). In his later expositions of his theory, he dropped even this
primordial artifice. But it served its purpose to show that, in his view,
economic instability is associated with the emergence of money and
credit. (In his later years, he made the following admission: 'I thought
that the alternations of good and bad trade must be of interest to all who
concerned themselves with public affairs. The method of exposition
starting with a simplified model, and dropping the simplified hypotheses
one after another, was intended for this wider circle.')[24]

In his next book, *Currency and Credit*, first published in 1919, Hawtrey
extended this analysis. By 'currency' he meant metallic money and the
notes issued by the central bank, while credit meant essentially deposits
with the commercial banks. Currency of course circulates around the
economy. But an 'unspent margin' is paid into banks or held as what
would now be called money balances. Somewhat confusingly, Hawtrey
includes in the 'unspent margin' all credit available in the economy.[25] But
this was to show that his theory is consistent with the Quantity Theory
of Money: '... given all the other economic conditions, the price level is
proportional to the unspent margin'.[26] If the theories are consistent then it
is only by ignoring the main conclusions of Hawtrey's analysis, described
in his words above, that fluctuations in money and credit are the cause of
economic instability, rather than proportional changes in prices. Credit
was more than just a factor in instability. When spent, credit is trans-
formed into income, and income then determines expenditure, for which
he used the term 'effective demand' that later became associated with
Keynes's critique of the 'classics' who adhered to Say's Law.[27] However,
he insisted that 'in the long run' income is equal to expenditure.[28] Hence
'saving' was not a problem which he admitted to his system. But his
insistence that credit creates incomes marked an important step away
from the Quantity Theory of Money.[29]

According to Hawtrey, the amount of currency in bank tills determines
the amount of credit which banks may advance. However, they cannot
induce borrowers to borrow from them. All that they can do is to vary the
rate of interest on their loans in the hope of attracting borrowers, or discouraging them if the commercial banks wish to conserve their currency,
or raise the cash ratio which is crucial for their ability to pay currency on

demand against deposits. But the amount of currency which the banks have in their tills depends on four factors. The first of these is the amount of bank-notes issued by the central bank and the amount of gold bullion in the country which, under the gold standard rules, determined the note issue of the central bank. After the First World War Hawtrey advocated cooperation between central banks to stabilise credit and the foreign exchange markets. He represented the British Treasury at the Genoa Conference on international monetary cooperation in 1922.[30] Later on, following the collapse of the gold standard and the onset of the Great Depression of the 1930s, Hawtrey advocated open market operations (the purchase of government bonds), as a way of improving the liquidity of the banking system, and low interest rates as means of reviving trade.[31] A second influence on the liquidity of the banking system that is rarely mentioned in discussions of Hawtrey is the distribution of income. In Hawtrey's time, only the rich, and businesses using credit, had bank accounts which they used for payments. Hawtrey was a pioneer in monetary economics in recognising that the use of bank accounts in payments was a way of economising on currency. A corollary of this was that the more workers were employed in an enterprise, the more currency they took out of the banking system.[32]

The third and, in Hawtrey's original view, the most important factor influencing the liquidity of the banking system was the amount of activity in the economy, which determined the proportion of currency issued that was circulating outside the banks. Here the crucial part was played by retail or wholesale 'traders' who financed their stocks with bank credit. If interest rates increased, traders were induced to economise on their use of credit by reducing the stocks of goods that they held. They could not do this by increasing sales (since that is a decision for their customers), but they could reduce orders to producers. Lower orders and falling prices would reduce the rate of profit. Output employment and income would be reduced. Unemployment would then last for as long as it took wages to fall until the rate of profit was restored. With a given amount of currency in the economy, production and exchange at lower wages and prices would cause an accumulation of cash in bank tills. Banks would then lower the rate of interest to stimulate borrowing.[33]

A fourth factor increasingly preoccupied Hawtrey during the inter-war period: International trade under the gold standard meant periodic shipments of gold bullion between trading countries.[34] Under the gold standard, a fall in gold reserves due to excessive imports obliged the central bank to reduce the number of its bank-notes in issue. This was sometimes done by the sale of government bonds. Such open market operations would drain the currency from banks, causing them to cease lending and raise their rate of interest to attract currency deposits and discourage borrowing. More commonly, the central bank would raise the rate of interest at which it discounted bills, known in Britain as the Bank Rate, allowing the central bank to issue less paper money in exchange for a nominal amount of bills. The First World War had a devastating effect on the distribution of gold reserves around the world, concentrating them in the creditor countries, principally the United States. The belligerent countries restricted their gold payments and for six years after hostilities ceased British governments and their advisers wrestled with the problem of how to return to full gold convertibility with prices, wages and a currency issue inflated by war expenditure. Britain's return to the gold standard at the pre-war parity was finally achieved in 1925, setting off a litany of complaints by manufacturers, reiterated periodically through the rest of the century, that they were being priced out of their export markets by the exchange rate. With the collapse of the US market, following the 1929 Crash, the gold standard was blamed for the trade crisis, both because of the high value of sterling that it required in relation to other currencies and because of the high bank rate required to maintain sterling's parity with gold. In 1931, Britain finally abandoned the gold standard. But Hawtrey remained convinced that the 1930s Depression was caused by the earlier high interest rates.

4.2   UNSTABLE FINANCE: THE CLASH WITH KEYNES

The vicissitudes of the currency, at a time of economic instability and depression, confirmed Hawtrey's conviction that money causes economic fluctuations, a view that was to be echoed by a later generation of monetarist economists.[35] In the case of the US stock market speculation, Hawtrey like Keynes associated it with a boom in fixed capital investment attendant upon a fall in the long-term rate of interest. However, in an interesting anticipation (of which both parties were unaware) of Kalecki's Principle of Increasing Risk and the later theories that companies use stock markets to refinance successful fixed capital investment,[36] Hawtrey pointed out that 'Resources for new investment are derived mainly from profits ... a large proportion of the capital has been supplied not by issues in the market at all, but by the limitation of dividends and the retention of a large proportion of profits in the form of reserves.'[37]

Hawtrey argued that there was virtually no net increase in capital issues by industrial and commercial companies. With rising profits, companies could obtain a higher return by lending money to brokers rather than placing it on deposit with banks. Brokers' loans, or 'call money' fuelled the speculation on the stock market until the Federal Reserve raised its rediscount rate from 3.5 per cent in three stages in the first half of 1928 in order to reduce the speculation, but also to stop an outflow of gold from the United States. It was finally raised to 6 per cent in August 1929. Meanwhile, the rate of interest on 'call money' had risen from 4.24 per cent at the beginning of 1928 to 9.23 per cent in July 1929, just prior to the Crash. When prices collapsed, the effect on speculators' incomes was to reduce their spending power. The collapse was made worse by the failure of the Federal Reserve to reduce interest rates sufficiently after the Crash.[38] The subsequent depression could only be effectively combated by a policy of cheap credit and open market operations in the principal gold-holding country, the United States, to force currency into circulation by buying in bonds.

By 1931, Hawtrey was urging 'that the fall of wages should *overtake* the fall of prices', which he thought would be sufficient to give a country a competitive advantage in trade.[39] The problem with this was that if all industrial countries reduced wages together, none would gain any advantage. In a rather confused passage he concluded that 'decisive action still rests with the banking system – that is to say, with the central banks of the world'.[40] He nevertheless returned with an emphasis that seems almost visceral 'As to unemployment, that need not increase greatly *provided* workpeople all over the world are willing to acquiesce at short intervals in prompt and large cuts in wages.'[41] This and his opposition to deficit spending by the British government (the notorious 'Treasury View') made him reviled by Liberals and Socialists alike.[42] There was a greater consistency to his analysis than they would often allow. His opposition to fiscal stimulus in Britain was not one of principle, but was consistent with his belief that such action was either unnecessary, if sufficient credit was available in the financial system to finance the government's deficit, or would threaten the gold and foreign currency reserves held by the central bank. These would be depleted by the increase in imports that would come with an economic recovery in Britain. Only the United States had sufficiently strong gold reserves to be able to sustain an economic recovery.[43]

In addition to his hint of later developments of Kalecki's Principle of Increasing Risk Hawtrey appears to have become convinced by the 1929

Stock Market Crash that the stock market is not permanently in that state of equilibrium so beloved of later financial economists. He argued that the relevant measure of supply and demand was the placing of new issues and their purchase by investors out of their savings. Echoing Wicksell's analysis of the capital market, Hawtrey saw the balance between supply and demand in it as made up by the borrowing of brokers, or their repayment of loans:

> The new issues will not be exactly equal to the savings. If they exceed the savings in any interval of time, the excess has to be held by the dealers in the investment market (stock jobbers) and they have to borrow money for the purpose. If the new issues fall short of savings, the dealers in the market receive more money than they pay out, and are enabled to repay bank advances.[44]

In addition to their later polemics about fiscal activism, Hawtrey and Keynes conducted an extensive correspondence on economic and monetary theory. The account of this that is given below is necessarily selective. A fuller account is given by Patrick Deutscher in his book *R.G. Hawtrey and the Development of Macroeconomics*. Deutscher's two chapters on Keynes and Hawtrey confirm that much of the difference between them was terminological, or was perceived as such by them. An inordinate amount of their correspondence consists of detailed explanation of terms which they themselves had invented. Keynes and Hawtrey had disagreed when the latter presented evidence to the Macmillan Committee on Finance and Industry in 1930, of which Keynes was a member. Their initial differences over terminology crystallised into a fundamental divergence concerning the importance of the short-term rate of interest in the economy. In Volume I of his *Treatise on Money* Keynes dismissed the idea that low interest rates stimulated 'speculation' in commodities. He quoted with approval Thomas Tooke's refutation nearly a century earlier of Joseph Hume's view that lower interest rates encouraged such excess: 'It is not the mere facility of borrowing, or the difference between being able to discount at 3 or at 6 per cent that supplies the *motive* for purchasing or even for selling', but the difference between the expected rate of profit on the speculation and the rate of interest on the borrowing that finances it.[45] Keynes went on to argue that the stocks held by traders did not vary, as Hawtrey argued, inversely with their working capital, and were in fact much more modest than Hawtrey supposed. Moreover, Keynes argued, the interest cost of stocks was 'perhaps the least important' of their expenses, by comparison with the deterioration in their quality, warehouse costs and the risk of price changes.[46]

Keynes's criticisms were echoed by his disciple Nicholas Kaldor, who cited the 1959 Radcliffe Report on the Working of the Monetary System to dispose of Hawtrey with the argument that 'stocks of commodities are extremely insensitive to interest rates'.[47] This was a characteristic over-simplification of Hawtrey's view that traders' *desired* rather than their *actual* stocks vary with the rate of interest. In the fourth, 1950, edition of his *Currency and Credit* Hawtrey inserted on page 69 a paragraph arguing that, in response to an increase in short-term interest rates, 'it is very easy for the trader to reduce the average quantity of goods held in stock, and so his indebtedness to the banker'. But this would always depend on the volume of demand. In his earliest work, he stated that 'traders' attempts to reduce stocks to economise on interest charges will be frustrated by reduced demand in a recession'.[48] Stocks were important for Hawtrey, not so much because they varied with the business cycle, but because attempts to reduce them transmitted to industry, and eventually consumers, the effects in lower orders of higher interest rates. It was Hawtrey who gave Keynes the idea that a fall in investment, relative to planned saving would result, initially at least, in a rise in stocks of unsold goods.[49] Such a fall in investment, in Keynes's analysis, would be associated with a rise in rates of interest, relative to the marginal efficiency of capital, the prospective return on the investment of new capital.[50] In such circumstances, higher stocks would be associated, temporarily at least, with a higher relative rate of interest. In his contribution to the symposium in the *Economic Journal* on 'Alternative Theories of the Rate of Interest' Hawtrey again referred to the possibility that excessive stocks may be expected, but the trader may be unable to prevent them from accumulating.

Kaldor's view, echoing Keynes's early criticism, thus did not take into account the qualifications that Hawtrey made in his analysis of the business cycle to his view of stocks as a monetary transmission mechanism. Kaldor's alternative view of money, the theory that money supply is 'endogenous' or determined by the level of activity in the economy, is largely consistent with Hawtrey's view that credit supply is elastic as long as banks have sufficient reserves.[51]

Hawtrey responded by criticising Keynes's over-simplified idea that the long-term or bond rate of interest moves up and down with the money rate of interest: 'There is no fixed relation between the average short-term rate and the long-term rate, and expectations regarding the short-term rate depend on circumstances. Such expectations, when they extend beyond a few months, are extremely conjectural. The short-term rate also may *exceed* the long-term rate.'[52] Hawtrey seems to have persuaded Keynes to moderate his optimism that the long-term rate of interest would respond readily to changes in the short-term Bank Rate. By this time, Hawtrey's studies had revealed to him the relative stability of the long-term rate of interest.[53] Hawtrey concluded that long-term finance for investment from the stock market was rationed, rather than regulated by the interest or dividend yield on securities:

> ... the volume of capital outlay is remarkably insensitive to the rate of interest, and in practice equilibrium is preserved in the investment market, at any rate over short periods, rather by a system of refusing to float more enterprises than the market can absorb than by varying the rate of interest.[54]

However, underlying their difference over which was the crucial rate of interest, the long-term, or the short-term one, lay a profounder difference over which was the crucial variable transmitting changes in the rate of interest to the economy as a whole. For Keynes it was investment in fixed capital. For Hawtrey it was stocks. It was Hawtrey rather than Keynes whose theory was considered to be disproved by empirical studies conducted by Jan Tinbergen and, in Oxford, P.W.S. Andrews and his associates. These concluded that interest rates had very little effect on business investment in either stocks or fixed capital.[55] But, in retrospect and unacknowledged, Hawtrey may have won the battle for the hearts and minds of the economics profession. The interpretation of Keynes that took over after Keynes's death was essentially a Hawtreyan one, of a credit economy (monetary production economy) regulated by fiscal policy and monetary policy concentrating increasingly on short-term interest rates and control of the money supply.[56] A generation of economists were taught their 'Keynesian' economics in the form, popularised by John Hicks and Paul Samuelson, of an IS/LM model of equilibrium in the goods market and the money market, an equilibrium that was between money market rates of interest and equilibrium between saving and investment.[57] An important difference is that, in the last quarter of the twentieth century in the main industrialised countries, what Hawtrey termed 'currency', i.e. notes and coins, ceased to be important for anything other than marginal or black market transactions as only a small minority of poorer citizens remain operating without a bank account. Another important difference is that monetary conditions are now thought to influence investment in fixed capital directly, rather than through changes in stocks.

In putting forward this Hawtreyan credit economy in the form of a Keynesian 'short-period' equilibrium it was also conveniently forgotten that Hawtrey presented an explanation of economic instability in a credit economy prior to the emergence of finance/capital markets as determining fluctuations in a capitalist economy. Arguably, Hawtrey's view of the capitalist economy was essentially the banking economy that Britain was for most of the nineteenth century. This has to be borne in mind when examining the work of the twentieth-century economists who took up his ideas selectively, principally Milton Friedman.

Hawtrey's analysis of emerging capitalism reliant on banks for finance still has relevance to the developing countries and Newly Industrialised Countries, where finance has yet to mature. In those countries, the credit system faces a similar constraint to that analysed by Hawtrey under the gold standard. However, that constraint on credit is not the amount of gold held in the economy, but the amount of convertible currencies, chiefly the dollar. Credit in the developing and semi-industrialised countries is therefore obliged to expand and contract with fluctuations in foreign currency inflows and reserves. The system is supposedly regulated by the central banks using Hawtrey's recommended instruments of open market operations and the short-term rate of interest. With outflows of foreign currency reserves, interest rates are raised, and credit is contracted in the kind of deflationary crisis that was familiar to Hawtrey, and has come to be familiar to us from events in Mexico in 1995, East Asia in 1997–1998, Russia in 1998, and Turkey in 2001.

Modern times have, however, added a dimension that was not available at the time of the gold standard, when Hawtrey developed his analysis. At that time for countries on the gold standard the exchange rate was fixed, and the only way out was to suspend the convertibility of central bank-notes against gold. The inflexibility of these arrangements was recognised in the Bretton Woods arrangements allowing a change in the exchange rate under exceptional circumstances. After the breakdown of these arrangements, depreciation of the exchange rate came to be widely used as a means of obtaining competitive advantage in export markets, but also to economise on foreign currency reserves: for a given amount of domestic currency which investors and importers wish to convert into foreign currency, the central bank has to supply less foreign currency out of its reserves. In developing countries where credit is increasingly influenced by the amount of foreign currency reserves, depreciation has therefore come to be a means of economising on bank reserves. These were problems which the main capitalist countries struggled with during the 1930s. In the limit, under a currency board system, credit is only determined by such reserves, depreciation is not allowed, and the only way of supporting the exchange rate is in the gold standard way, by offering a higher rate of interest for foreign currency deposits with the central bank. The currency board therefore corresponds to a modern kind of gold standard with all the dangers of banking and economic instability which Hawtrey had exposed.

This issue with implications for banking at the end of the twentieth century had been raised by the American economist Alvin Hansen, who went on to become a distinguished exponent of Keynes's views in the United States. Prior to his conversion by Keynes, Hansen had adhered to Hawtrey's views on the monetary business cycle. However, he noted that Hawtrey's business cycle arose because the expansion of credit is followed by a drain of reserves from the banking system, and banks have no other way of regulating their reserves than by raising their interest rates.

In one other respect Hawtrey looked forward to later theoretical developments. In his earlier-cited criticism of Keynes's *General Theory*, Hawtrey argued that Keynes was wrong to overlook the internal liquidity of industrial and commercial companies in his analysis of the speculative demand for money:

> It is curious that Mr. Keynes seems to limit the scope of the function $L_2(r)$ to an *individual* disposing of saving (current or past) out of income ... It is reasonable to suppose that the omission of redundant cash accumulated by business concerns is accidental, and that he would include the idle working capital of a business in the idle balances.[58]

Anxious to rehabilitate his traders' role in transmitting the effects of credit expansions and contractions to the rest of the economy, Hawtrey himself overlooked the fact that businesses possess liquidity over and above their working capital. This is the liquid reserves out of which they finance their fixed capital investment or which they hold as security against excess financial liabilities. The analysis of the economic consequences of such internal finance was developed from the 1930s onwards by Marek Breit, Michał Kalecki and Josef Steindl as the Principle of Increasing Risk relating the business cycle to corporate finance in the modern form of finance capitalism.

NOTES

1. Gilbert 1982, p. 235; Hicks 1977, p. 118 and note 3.
2. An exception here is David Laidler: 'Marshall and Pigou ... [contributed] to the understanding of certain characteristics of the upswing and the downswing phases of the cycle, and the monetary elements at work in them, [rather] than ... creating a coherent model of the cycle taken as a whole. It was Ralph Hawtrey ... who ... produced a complete and purely monetary theory of the cycle. He integrated the cash balance approach to the quantity theory with other elements in Cambridge thought, not to mention some acute insights of his own, into a theory of fluctuations which explained turning points as endogenous phenomena. Unlike Fisher, moreover, Hawtrey treated output and employment fluctuations as essential features of the cycle.' Laidler 1991, pp. 100–101.
3. Roll 1960, p. 458.
4. Schumpeter 1954, p. 1121.
5. Klein 1947, p. 103.
6. Hawtrey 1931; see also Hawtrey 1925.
7. Victoria Chick takes a somewhat different view on equilibrium in Keynes in 'Equilibrium and Determination in Open Systems' (Chick 1996). Her view would bring Keynes methodologically closer to Hawtrey.
8. Deutscher 1990, p. 243.
9. Ibid. Susan Howson argues that his policy advice had fallen out of favour even during the 1930s, after the British government took up public works, which Hawtrey had opposed, and adopted cheap money with a 2 per cent Bank Rate, which he had advocated. Howson 1985.
10. Hawtrey 1961, p. xxii.
11. Hayek 1935; Friedman 1986; Friedman and Schwartz 1963.
12. Lucas 1981.
13. Wojnilower 1980 and 1985.
14. Friedman 1968.
15. Laidler points out that Wicksell's work was not available to English readers until the 1930s. See Laidler 1999, pp. 13–14.
16. Wicksell 1898.
17. See Keynes's review of Fisher's *The Purchasing Power of Money*, Keynes 1911, and Keynes 1913. These are further discussed in Chapter 7.
18. Marshall and Marshall 1879, Book III, chapters 1 and 2. See also Eshag 1963 and Gootzeit 1999.
19. Towards the end of his life, Hawtrey admitted that when he wrote his first book, in 1909, 'I had read very little economics' (Hawtrey 1961, p. viii) – not bad, one must admit, for someone who had by then been employed as an economist at the British Treasury for five years! Susan Howson informs me that Hawtrey said that he learned a great deal from his Treasury superior Sir John Bradbury 'whose knowledge of British financial institutions was unparalleled outside the City of London at that time'. However, he only joined Bradbury in the Finance Division of the Treasury five years *after* starting at the Treasury (Howson 1985, pp. 144–145). Still, the standards of

his superior may account for Hawtrey's fastidious admission in 1961 that his first book 'exposed my ignorance of the functions of bill-brokers', with page number references where this was revealed (Hawtrey 1961, p. ix).

20. Cited in Corry 1962, p. 85.
21. Hawtrey 1913, p. 199.
22. Hawtrey 1931, p. 10.
23. Hawtrey 1934, p. 58.
24. Hawtrey 1961, p. ix.
25. Hawtrey 1934, pp. 34–55.
26. Ibid., pp. 34–35.
27. Hawtrey 1913, p. 6.
28. Ibid., p. 34.
29. Realfonzo 1998, pp. 19–20. Laidler (1999, pp. 112–120) gives a more monetarist interpretation.
30. See Howson 1985 for references.
31. Hawtrey 1931.
32. Hawtrey 1934, pp. 42–43.
33. Hawtrey 1913, pp. 44–46.
34. Ibid., Chapter IX.
35. E.g. Capie, Mills and Wood 1986 and Bordo 1986.
36. Anderson 1964; Toporowski 2000, Chapter 1.
37. Hawtrey 1938, p. 49. Such views had also appeared in the Report of the Macmillan Committee, to which Hawtrey had contributed.
38. Hawtrey 1933, pp. 79–80.
39. Hawtrey 1931, p. 44.
40. Ibid., pp. 44–45.
41. Ibid., p. 83.
42. 'Soon after "Good and Bad Trade" appeared, F.H. Keeling, an intellectual Socialist, reproached me with having recommended reductions of wages. I disavowed having made any such recommendation, though I had contended that prompt and appropriate changes in wages, upward as well as downward, would counteract the injurious consequences of the cycle … Discussion elicited the fact that he was quite unaware that the supply of gold set a limit beyond which the wage level would cause increases in unemployment.' Hawtrey 1961, p. x.
43. Hawtrey 1931, pp. 61–84. Later in life he argued that his first book 'puts forward changes in the wage level as an alternative to adopting an inconvertible paper currency, subject to a system of banking control which would effectively prevent fluctuations being generated in the country itself'. Hawtrey 1961, p. x.
44. Hawtrey 1931, p. 8. See also Hawtrey 1938, pp. 62–63.
45. Keynes 1930, Vol. I, pp. 174–175.
46. Keynes was speaking from his own experience of speculation in commodities. In 1936 he even considered the possibility of using the Chapel of King's College Cambridge, of which he was Bursar, to store a large quantity of wheat which he feared he may have to take delivery of. Harrod 1951, pp. 294–304; Keynes 1983, pp. 10–11.

47. Kaldor 1982, p. 7. See also Kaldor 1938.
48. Hawtrey 1913, p. 62.
49. Deutscher 1990, pp. 108–109.
50. Keynes 1936, pp. 317–318.
51. On their own, theories of monetary endogeneity may be a form of 'reflective finance', as long as they ignore the other (more implicit) part of Keynes's criticism of Hawtrey, namely that the long-term rate of interest, rather than the short-term one, prevents the economy from moving into a full employment equilibrium.
52. Hawtrey 1937, p. 191.
53. Ibid., p. 114.
54. Ibid., p. 188.
55. Deutscher 1990, pp. 224–228.
56. Laidler 1999.
57. Chick 1983, pp. 3–4.
58. Hawtrey 1937, p. 219.

5. Irving Fisher and debt deflation

Until recently, the views of Irving Fisher (1867–1947) on finance have tended to be obscured by the blow that his reputation suffered after his pronouncement, on the eve of the 1929 Crash, that 'stock prices have reached what looks like a permanently high plateau'.[1] Shortly after the Crash, he published a book entitled *The Stock Market Crash – And After*, in which he argued that the stock market boom that preceded the Crash was justified by structural improvements that had taken place in the US economy during the 1920s. Mergers and acquisitions, he felt, allowed economies of scale to take place, along with scientific breakthroughs and innovations. The 'scientific management' movement of Taylorism, improved lay-out of manufacturing plants, and a greater cooperation of trades unions in industrial management, were also destined to increase the productivity of business, and the earnings of stock-holders.[2]

However, Fisher was a much more thoughtful commentator on economic developments than Galbraith's selective quotations, and Fisher's initial response to the Crash, would suggest. When he had reconciled himself to the loss in the Crash of his sister's wealth, which she had placed under his management, Fisher reflected on a possible connection between the financial inflation that had caused him this loss, and the Great Depression that followed. In 1931, in the course of his lectures at Yale, he first enunciated his theory of debt deflation. He wrote up his reflections and analysis on business in his book *Booms and Depressions*.[3] By way of highlighting his distinctive views on the subject, he distilled his main conclusions from that book into a paper on 'The Debt Deflation Theory of Great Depressions' which was published in a memorable first issue of *Econometrica*.[4]

Fisher's paper is extraordinary, not only for the originality of his theory, but also because it belies the commonly held view that, as a mathematical economist, he was somehow a 'fellow-traveller' of the neo-classical, equilibrium school of economics. He had already advanced a credit cycle theory in his 1907 book, *The Rate of Interest*. However, these cycles were not caused by the autonomous operations of the credit system, but by the limited outlook and perceptions of borrowers and lenders. This causes them to make future financial commitments without knowing what the future price level will be, with the result that the real value of debts can change. Such changes then cause fluctuations in investment as well as redistributing wealth between borrowers and lenders:

> ... periods of speculation and depression are the result of *inequality* of fore-sight ... *imperfection* of foresight transfers wealth from creditor to debtor, or the reverse, *inequality* of foresight produces over-investment during rising prices, and relative stagnation during falling prices. In the former case society is trapped into devoting too much investment of productive energies for future return, while in the contrary case, under-investment is the rule.[5]

In 1933 he pointed out right at the start of his paper that equilibrium is an imaginary state of affairs: 'Only in imagination can all ... variables remain constant and be kept in equilibrium by the balanced forces of human desires, as manifested through "supply and demand".'[6] Business cycles are part of economic dynamics which occur because of 'economic dis-equilibrium'. Therefore no two cycles are the same.

Fisher argued that cycles occur because of inconsistencies at any one time between a whole range of variables, such as investment, the capital stock, and industrial and agricultural prices. But serious 'over-speculation' and crises are caused by the interaction between debt and 'the purchasing power of the monetary unit':

> Disturbances in these two factors ... will set up serious disturbances in all, or nearly all, other economic variables. On the other hand, if debt and deflation are absent, other disturbances are powerless to bring on crises comparable in severity to those of 1837, 1873, or 1929–1933.[7]

This identification of two crucial monetary and financial variables with a virtually all-pervasive destabilising effect on a (credit) economy was to be developed in the 1970s by Hyman P. Minsky in his Financial Instability Hypothesis. 'A capitalist economy ... is characterised by two sets of relative prices, one of current output and the other of capital assets.' The first of these determines money incomes. The second determines assets, liabilities. 'The alignment of these two sets of prices determines investment and the evolution of an economy over time.'[8] This distinction between the price system of the financial markets and the price system in the markets for goods and services is a crucial difference between the respective analyses of Fisher and Minsky, and that of Keynes. Bertil Ohlin, an early sympathetic critic of the *General Theory* pointed out that 'Keynes's construction ... seems to regard the rate of interest as determined "outside" the price system, or at least as having almost no connection with the system of mutually interdependent prices and quantities.'[9]

Fisher argued that debt deflation was set off by over-indebtedness. The latter was commonly set off by over-borrowing, due to too low interest rates raising the temptation 'to borrow, and invest or speculate with borrowed money'. Commonly this is associated with 'new opportunities to invest at a big prospective profit'. Thus over-borrowing may be induced by inventions and technological improvements, war debts and reconstruction loans to foreign countries. But 'easy money is the great cause of over-borrowing' and Fisher mentions 'the low interest policy adopted to help England get back on the gold standard in 1925' as a factor.[10]

Once over-borrowing takes hold, borrowers try to reduce their debt by increasing sales of their assets. This distress selling causes prices to fall. Falling prices in turn raise the real value of money ('a swelling of the dollar') and in turn the value of debts denominated in nominal terms. A paradoxical situation develops in which, the more borrowers try to reduce their debt, the more it grows. The result is a process whereby debt reduces the velocity of circulation of bank deposits, causing a fall in the level of prices, falling profits and bankruptcies. Falling output and employment in turn lead to pessimism and hoarding which further slows down the velocity of circulation.

This was Fisher's explanation of the 1930s economic depression. Two possible solutions to the depression were possible. The 'natural' one occurs when, 'after almost universal bankruptcy, the indebtedness must cease to grow greater and begin to grow less'. The recovery that followed would enable debt to start growing again, opening the way for the next bout of over-borrowing. However, waiting for such a spontaneous recovery involved 'needless and cruel bankruptcy, unemployment, and starvation'.[11] A far better way is to reflate the economy. Fisher mentioned the open market policies pursued by the Federal Reserve under President Hoover as reviving prices and business in the summer of 1932. He also suggested that deficit spending could help.

After the Second World War, Fisher's analysis failed to attract mainstream interest in the economics profession. A rather obvious reason is the crucial role in it of falling prices ('swelling of the dollar'). Until recently, in the main industrialised countries with sophisticated financial systems, prices have not fallen since the Second World War. If anything they rose. Fisher's analysis was overshadowed by Keynes's more sophisticated explanation of depression, and languished in obscurity until Minsky discovered it in the 1940s and made it the starting point of his reinterpretation of Keynes.

More crucially, Fisher himself shifted his point of view later in the 1930s towards a more purely monetarist explanation of the depression. In a public lecture at the Cowles Commission annual research conference at Colorado College on 10 July 1936, Fisher argued that, among all the factors contributing to the Depression, 'one cause towers above all the other, the collapse of our deposit currency. The depression was a money famine – a famine, not of pocket-book money but of check-book money ... our deposits subject to check. In 1929, our check-book money amounted to 23 billion dollars. In 1933, before our "bank holiday" it was only 15 billions ...'.[12] It was this monetarist explanation of the Depression that was subsequently reiterated by Milton Friedman in his monetarist *Monetary History of the United States 1867–1960*.

NOTES

1. Galbraith 1980, p. 70. Laidler notes that 'Because Fisher had publicly expressed his faith in the durability of the stock market boom in September 1929, had persisted in pronouncing the market's subsequent collapse temporary well into 1930, and had also found time in 1930 to publish a defence of Prohibition ... it is not surprising that he found himself thus placed in the company of monetary cranks.' Laidler 1999, p. 229.
2. Fisher 1930.
3. Fisher 1932.
4. Note 4 of that article details the development of his theory and, prompted by Wesley Mitchell, acknowledges that Veblen, in Chapter VII of *Theory of Business Enterprise*, 'comes nearest to the debt deflation theory'.
5. Fisher 1907, pp. 285–287. Fisher was nothing if not consistent in his analysis during this period. Exactly the same passage is reproduced on exactly the same numbered pages in his 1911 book *The Purchasing Power of Money*.
6. Fisher 1933, p. 337.
7. Fisher 1933, p. 341.
8. Minsky 1978, p. 5.
9. Ohlin 1937. This is precisely why Schumpeter described Keynes's theory as 'a monetary theory of interest, according to which interest is not derived from, or expressive of, anything that has, in whatever form, to do with the net return from capital goods'. In a footnote appended to this remark, Schumpeter commented: '... this is, speaking from the standpoint of theoretical analysis alone, perhaps the most important original contribution of the *General Theory* ...' (Schumpeter 1954, p. 1178).
10. Fisher 1933, p. 348.
11. Fisher 1933, p. 348.

12. Fisher 1936, quoted in Dimand 2000.

6. John Maynard Keynes's financial theory of under-investment: towards doubt

As an exponent of critical finance John Maynard Keynes requires a degree of reinterpretation. Hyman P. Minsky recognised that Keynes's analysis of how finance disturbs the capitalist economy needs to be retrieved from the neo-classical makeover of his views that appears in economics textbooks. (For example, in the Hicks-Hansen IS/LM system, finance is reduced to the money markets of an economy.) On closer examination, it turns out that Keynes's views may not have been evolving in quite the direction which Minsky perceived in them.[1] The interpretation given in this chapter and the next is perhaps more consistent with that of Keynes's contemporaries, most notably his friend, rival and correspondent on monetary and policy issues, Ralph Hawtrey.[2] Keynes's purpose, as he made clear in the closing paragraphs of his *General Theory*, beginning with the question 'is the fulfilment of these ideas a visionary hope' (and continuing '… the power of vested interests is vastly exaggerated compared with the gradual encroachment of ideas … it is ideas, not vested interests, which are dangerous for good or evil'[3]), was to change the ideas of policy-makers, academics, and the educated public. This rhetorical, *ad hominem* aspect of his exposition accounts for much of the incoherence which his critics observed, and continue to find, in his analysis. His style, his championing at various times of ideas which were not necessarily consistent with each other, and his own notorious apostasy from views previously advocated, make Keynesian exegesis a particularly fruitful, if treacherous, endeavour and afford a modicum of validity to different interpretations.[4]

6.1   KEYNES'S EARLY VIEWS ON FINANCE

Keynes's early views on finance were little distinct from the views of his Cambridge teacher Alfred Marshall. Marshall's views on the role of credit in the business cycle, as expressed in his early book (co-authored with his wife Mary Paley Marshall) *The Economics of Industry*, and in his later work *Money, Credit and Commerce* is another instance of his broadly equilibrium approach to finance. An 'easing' of credit, the willingness of banks to lend more at interest rates below prospective rates of profit in particular lines of business, stimulates business activity and inflationary speculation. The need to sell speculatively purchased or produced goods to repay debts (or avoid losses), or higher interest rates, then brings the boom to an end. Such speculative booms are propagated internationally by the rise in imports that occurs with increased business activity. Marshall's views on this remained largely unchanged from the earlier views of John Stuart Mill, and changed little over the span of Marshall's own work. Indeed, the account he gave in *Money, Credit and Commerce*, which he first published in 1924 but drafted much earlier, is much the same as the accounts given in his *Principles of Economics* and *Economics of Industry*.[5] Since the span of that work coincided with many of the dramas and crises in the financial markets that inspired Veblen's critique, it was not surprising that Marshall had views on financial speculation. But these turned out to be common wisdom, in their time and ours: Such speculation drove stock market values away from equilibrium values determined in the real economy by profits and saving, and gave windfall profits to traders in securities with 'inside' information, at the expense of 'outside' amateurs. All this Marshall felt, naturally enough, was morally deplorable. But it was deemed to be an aberration, so that its broader economic consequences were not considered.[6]

More recent research by Michael Lawlor has revealed that, in addition to Marshall, the other influence on Keynes's early thought on finance was the work of a now obscure American lawyer, who dabbled in financial economics, Henry Crosby Emery. In Cambridge before the First World War, Keynes lectured on 'Modern Business Methods' and 'The Stock Exchange and the Money Market'. Curiously, he listed as reading recommended to his students Veblen's *Theory of Business Enterprise*, where Veblen advanced an account of speculation in conditions of uncertainty as the driving force of credit cycles. But his lectures drew most heavily on Emery's book *Speculation on the Stock and Produce Exchanges of the United States*.[7]

Emery put forward a theory that, in its essentials, was to be advanced during the 1970s as market efficiency theory. This reflects perhaps less the way in which economists ignorant of the history of economic thought acquire spurious originality by rediscovering the ideas of 'defunct economists', and more the way in which certain attitudes prevail during particular financial conjunctures. Emery was concerned to show that the sophisticated secondary and futures markets in the United States of the 1890s were performing a useful service. This was to provide arguments against attempts in the United States and in Germany to legislate in order to prevent what were regarded as speculative abuses in those markets. Emery was especially concerned with the futures contracts with which speculators made their profits and hedged their speculative positions. He argued that speculation had always accompanied trade, hence suggesting that constraints on speculation were likewise limitations on trade. However, according to Emery, speculation was 'limited to commodities of an uncertain production' and financial securities 'in the face of the many and hidden causes affecting value, involving the same uncertainties as the purchase of commodities under the new conditions of a world market'.[8] The role of uncertainty was crucial. Already in the 1890s the standard way of valuing stocks was by discounting future returns from them. If those returns are uncertain, then calculated speculation enters the market. Speculators were therefore necessary to provide certainty of future values to traders and industrialists faced with a risky and uncertain future. Indeed, speculation was essential to provide liquidity and establish equilibrium prices.

Emery therefore suggested that this warranted raising such activity to a fourth factor of production, after land, labour and capital. He detailed his analysis in a chapter with the suggestive title 'The Economic Function of Speculation'. In his chapter on 'Some Evils of Speculation' Emery argued that those evils were largely moral, while the benefits were largely economic: 'Even in the case of "gambling stocks" there is no need for the bona fide investor to be injured. His investment may be made elsewhere. The direct losses in the matter of these securities are borne by those speculators among the public who are foolish enough to tamper with such fraudulent schemes. Hence the economic evil is not great. The moral evil which results from the fact that such operators go unrebuked is of far greater consequence.'[9] Bourgeois propriety was maintained by making fraud the only pretext for regulation, because the benefits of arbitrage for all markets were so much greater.

Emery's explanation of how business involves commitments to future values, and how financial markets deal with uncertainty and risk, would have been philosophically congenial to the young Keynes who had just completed his *Treatise on Probability*. But Emery was not the only influence on Keynes. Frederick Lavington, a former bank employee, came to study economics at Cambridge in his late twenties, and attended

Keynes's Political Economy Club in Cambridge, until his untimely death in 1927. He had an insider's knowledge of the scandalous manipulations in the London Stock Exchange that followed the Boer War. He attended Keynes's lectures, and himself lectured at Cambridge during the 1920s. Lavington's conclusion on speculation was considerably more critical than that of Emery:

> ... there are considerable numbers of expert speculators who, in effect, deal through the Jobber with less well-informed members of the public and use their superior knowledge of securities or of moods of the public to transfer wealth from these other parties to themselves. The unskilled speculators and investors with whom they deal obtain some protection from the Jobber, and can, if they choose, obtain almost complete protection by acting only on the advice of a competent broker; but the facts show that they do not avail themselves fully of this safeguard. In so far as the expert speculator levies his toll from the speculating public without still further exciting their activities his operations are not without some advantage to society, for they tend to discourage the public from a form of enterprise which can rarely yield any net social advantage. In so far as he deals with investors he takes from them the advantage of price movements without giving any adequate return, and the *direct* effect of his operations is a net social loss.[10]

However, even in the Indian Summer of Edwardian capitalism before the First World War, Keynes showed an awareness of the crucial role that financial relations played in the generation of economic instability. In 1913, he presented a paper to the Political Economy Club with the provocative title of 'How Far are Bankers Responsible for the Alternations of Crisis and Depression'. In this paper Keynes put forward an explanation of how banks may make an economy fluctuate between over-investment in an economic boom and under-investment in a recession. Banks, he suggested, hold the 'free resources' or savings 'of the community'. These are lent out for business investment. But without control over the investment process, banks cannot prevent over-investment. When this requires even more credit to sustain it, banks call in loans and raise interest rates until loans are repaid regularly and promptly again. Thus it is not a shortage of cash, as Fisher and Hawtrey suggested, that causes banks to reduce their lending, but the illiquidity of loans committed to excessive investment.[11] At this stage, Keynes's thinking was clearly still rooted in something like a loanable funds analysis (banks are trying to equilibrate saving and investment indirectly by regulating the liquidity of their loans). The notion of an increasing illiquidity of investment was a feature of Austrian capital theory, but in Keynes's case was probably more the influence of Jevons. The latter's *The Theory of Political Economy* was the first economics book that Keynes read, and he had recently reviewed the fourth edition of that book.[12] The fundamental flaw in the analysis is Keynes's failure to grasp the principle of banking reflux. As investment proceeds, and even if it turns into over-investment in relation to saving or 'free resources', the payments made, with money borrowed or owned, for investment equipment delivered, is credited to their bank accounts as additional 'free resources' by the suppliers of investment equipment. In this way, the credit system inflates itself automatically in the course of an investment boom. Only when the investment boom breaks, and producers find themselves with equipment financed with bank credit, which they are unable to repay from the reduced proceeds of their output, do the banks find their loans becoming systematically illiquid. But the problem then arises in the real economy, and not in the banking system.

6.2   MANAGING THE CREDIT CYCLE

The development of Keynes's earlier thinking on the role played by finance in the capitalist economy came later and, as mentioned above, came as a by-product of his monetary analysis. In his *Treatise on Money*, whose proofs he revised in the wake of the 1929 Crash, Keynes, like Marshall and Fisher, distinguished between the financial circulation of money and its industrial circulation in order to refine the Quantity Theory of Money. This was necessary for his argument that saving may not always equal investment. But the 'credit cycle' which he put forward in the first volume of the *Treatise* turned out to be a Wicksellian cycle in which saving and investment diverge cyclically, as the actual rate of interest deviates cyclically from the 'natural' rate of interest. His interest was in the effect of this cycle on investment, prices and monetary circulation.[13] A 'bull' market in securities could coincide with over-investment, but only because the actual rate of interest would be below the natural rate of interest.[14]

As is well known, by the time he came to write his *General Theory*, Keynes's views had changed. But there was a core that had not changed. Already in the *Treatise on Money* Keynes had recognised that it was not the short-term, or money, rate of interest that affects the level of economic activity, but the long-term, or bond, rate of interest. Early on in the *Treatise* he disputed Hawtrey's claim that changes in the short-term rate of interest would influence the inclination of traders to speculate on the prospects of profit or higher prices.[15] In the second volume of the *Treatise*

Keynes included a chapter on 'The Control of the Rate of Investment'.[16] He introduced here the distinction between short-term rates of interest and long-term rates of interest. Keynes cited research published by the American economist Winfield William Riefler, whose conclusion he quoted: 'The surprising fact is not that bond yields are relatively stable in comparison with short-term rates, but rather that they have reflected fluctuations in short-term rates so strikingly and to such a considerable extent.'[17] Keynes then provided tables comparing the average Bank Rate and the yield on unredeemable government stocks ('consols') from 1906 to 1929 to argue that there are similarly synchronised movements of short-term and bond rate in the UK. 'It is rarely the case that bond yields will fail to rise (or fall) if the short-term rate remains at an absolutely higher (or lower) level than the bond yield even for a few weeks.'[18] This clearly implied a yield curve of relatively constant slope which moved up and down along its whole length in response to changes in the money market rate of interest. The relative stability of the slope of the yield curve was a crucial element in his analysis of monetary policy. However radically he changed his views on money in writing the *General Theory*, he retained basically the same view of the yield curve.[19]

In the *Treatise* Keynes argued that the relatively stable relationship between short-term rates and long-term rates was due to arbitrage by banks and financial institutions which would shift the composition of their portfolios towards bonds if the money market rates became too low. Rising bond prices would then reduce bond rates more or less correspondingly. Conversely, higher money market interest rates would cause these institutions to prefer the more liquid assets with higher returns, and the bear market would reduce bond prices and increase their implied yield.[20] Keynes appears to have been influenced here by the ideas of Frederick Lavington.[21] Richard Kahn, Keynes's closest research associate in the 1930s, suggested in the 1950s that the yield curve was formed by banks' regulating their liquidity by buying and selling government bonds, that is by the 'liquidity preference' of banks.[22] Keynes believed that while the effects of changes in money market rates of interest on working capital were likely to be small, '... the direct effects of cheap money operating through changes, even small ones, in the bond market ... is probably of more importance ...'. 'In the modern world, the volume of long-term borrowing for the purposes of new investment depends most directly on the attitude of the leading issue houses and underwriters' in the market for long-term securities.[23] Hence Keynes's remedy for persistent under-investment was for the central bank to buy long-term securities until the long-term rate of interest had fallen sufficiently low to stimulate new investment. This he believed would be effective because, in practice, only a small proportion of outstanding stock is actually turned over in the secondary market where the yield for securities is determined.[24] Furthermore, if the central bank supplied 'banks with more funds than they can lend at short-term, in the first place the short-term rate of interest will decline towards zero, and, in the second place, the member banks will soon begin, if only to maintain their profits, to second the efforts of the Central Bank by themselves buying securities'.[25]

Keynes admitted that buying of securities by a central bank may require them to be purchased 'at a price far beyond what it considers to the long-period norm' so that, 'when in due course they have to be reversed by sales at a later date, (they) may show a serious financial loss'. But, Keynes went on, 'this contingency ... can only arise as the result of inaccurate forecasting by the capitalist public and of a difference of opinion between the Central Bank and long-term borrowers as to the prospective rate of returns'.[26]

There is another difficulty, which Keynes did not mention perhaps because at this stage he still regarded the supply of central bank credit as having a fairly immediate impact on interest rates. Flooding the markets with more funds than banks can lend short-term merely reduces the excess demand for funds in the wholesale money markets. Usually this excess demand would be supplied by the central bank. If it is reduced then less will be supplied by the central bank at the request of banks and money-brokers (discount houses in Keynes's time). This would reduce the effect of the attempt to increase the supply of money. Even after any excess demand in the money markets may have been extinguished, the fear of capital loss in the market for longer-term securities may effectively prevent banks from buying such securities.

Keynes reinforced this view in three lectures which he contributed to a series organised by the Harris Foundation, at the University of Chicago in July 1931. Here he contrasted the experience of the United States during the 1920s, where investment activity was high, in spite of high interest rates, with the relatively lower investment activity in the UK. He argued that a decline in investment had started already in 1929, and, 'according to my theory, was the cause of the decline in business profits ...'.[27] The fall in investment was due to excessive interest rates, in relation to business profits. The very high interest rates in the United States brought gold into that country from the rest of the world, causing credit contraction in other countries.[28]

In these lectures, Keynes gave a revealing summary of the reflux theory of profits, and its connection to finance, that he had enunciated in his *Treatise on Money*:

> The costs of production of the entrepreneurs are equal to the incomes of the public. Now the incomes of the public are, obviously, equal to the sum of what they spend and of what they save. In the other hand, the sale proceeds of the entrepreneurs are equal to the sum of what the public spend on current consumption and what the financial machine is causing to be spent on current investment.
> Thus, the costs of the entrepreneurs are equal to what the public spend plus what they save; while the receipts of the entrepreneurs are equal to what the public spend plus the value of current investment. It follows ... that when the value of current investment is greater than the savings of the public, the receipts of the entrepreneurs are greater than their costs, so that they make a profit; and when, on the other hand, the value of current investment is less than the savings of the public, the receipts of the entrepreneurs will be less than their costs, so that they make a loss ...[29]

Keynes then reverted to an imbalance in the real economy as an explanation for economic disturbances: 'The whole matter may be summed up by saying that a boom is generated when investment exceeds saving, and a slump is generated when saving exceeds investment.'[30] Public works should be undertaken and confidence needed to be restored to lenders and borrowers, to raise investment and hence profits. Ultimately, 'the task of adjusting the long-term rate of interest to the technical possibilities of our age so that the demand for new capital is as nearly as possible equal to the community's current volume of savings must be the prime object of financial statesmanship'.[31]

Keynes recognised that this could not be done through the banking system, 'for prima facie the banking system is concerned with the short-term rate of interest rather than the long'. It had to be done by a combination of lowering the short-term rate of interest, open market operations, and restoring 'the attractions of non-liquid assets'.[32]

6.3   THE FAILURE OF MONETARY POLICY

The reflux theory of profits of the *Treatise on Money*, outlined in Chicago, was poorly received by his academic colleagues. Keynes abandoned it following discussions with his Cambridge acolytes, grouped informally in the Cambridge 'Circus' (see Chapter 10). More important, from the point of view of the development of his financial theory of investment, was the apparent failure of low interest rates to generate the predicted recovery of investment. In 1932 the Bank of England reduced its Bank Rate to an historic low which, however, failed to revive economic activity. On 30 June 1932, Bank Rate was cut to 2 per cent (it had been as high as 6 per cent when the Bank had suspended gold payments in 1931). Overnight loans in the money market fell to below 0.75 per cent. But the stock market revival was halting. In a rarely noted example of central bank open market operations designed to improve the liquidity of the market for long-term securities, the Bank also entered the market to buy government securities, prior to a conversion later that year of 5 per cent War Loans to 3.5 per cent. Similar measures of monetary expansion were undertaken in the United States and Europe. The net effect was to increase the liquidity of the banking system, with only a limited recovery in real investment,[33] an outcome that was widely regarded as confirming a causal link between liquidity preference in the financial markets, evidenced by the accumulation of unspent resources in the financial system, and under-investment in the real economy.

In June 1933, in an article published in the *American Economic Review*, Edward C. Simmons criticised Keynes's 'scheme for the control of the business cycle' by influencing the long-term rate of interest through manipulation of the short-term rate. Simmons argued that the relationship between the short-term and long-term rates of interest had been unstable in recent years, from 1928 to 1932, and therefore Keynes's 'scheme' would not work. Keynes replied by pointing out that the relationship between long- and short-term interest rates was by no means as unstable as Simmons suggested: '... even in these abnormal years the *directions* of changes in the two rates were the same'. Furthermore '... I am not one of those who believe that the business cycle can be controlled solely by manipulation of the short-term rate of interest ... I am indeed a strong critic of this view, and I have paid much attention to alternative and supplementary methods of controlling the rate of interest.'[34]

Keynes went on to argue that the influence of the short-term rate on the long-rate, while not 'infallible ... is not so negligible as one might have expected. ... My proposals for the control of the business cycle are based on the control of *investment*. ... I have been foremost to point out that circumstances can arise, and have arisen recently, when neither control of the short-term rate of interest nor even control of the long-term rate will be effective, with the result that direct stimulation of investment by government is the necessary means. Before a very abnormal situation has been allowed to develop, however, much milder methods, including control of the short-term rate of interest, may sometimes be sufficient, whilst they are seldom or never negligible.'[35]

By the mid-1930s, therefore, Keynes was entertaining doubts about the ability of the monetary authorities to control investment, and hence the business cycle, by acting upon the short-term rate of interest. As recently as 1930, he had confidently asserted that: 'A central bank, which is free to govern the volume of cash and reserve money in its monetary system by joint use of bank rate policy and open market operations, is master of the situation and is in a position to control not merely the volume of credit but the rate of investment, the level of prices and in the long run the level of incomes ...'.[36]

Keynes was now working on the drafts that were to become his *General Theory of Employment, Interest and Money*. In the course of his preparation, he had to uncover the reasons for the ineffectiveness of monetary and financial policy in bringing the economy to a more 'normal' situation, where such policy *could* bring about the desired levels of investment and employment. He did this by moving away from a business cycle methodology, in which the economic situation in a given period is explained by its antecedents in the previous period, or periods, towards short- and long-period equilibria. The characteristics of these equilibria were to be determined by generalised properties of commodities and individual human agents, with the short-term equilibrium dominating, but subsequent equilibria emerging through financing and capital commitments.

NOTES

1. Minsky 1975.
2. E.g. in Hawtrey 1962, pp. 196–198.
3. Keynes 1936, pp. 383–384.
4. His own acolytes recognised the enigmatic nature of Keynes's writing: Hicks famously detected 'at least three theories of money' in Keynes's *Treatise on Money* (Hicks 1935). In 1985, Geoffrey Harcourt and Terry O'Shaughnessy identified at least six different interpretations of the *General Theory* (Harcourt and O'Shaughnessy 1985). George Shackle aptly entitled his chapter on Keynes's own search to overcome the ambiguities of his *General Theory*, 'Keynes's Ultimate Meaning' (Shackle 1967).
5. Marshall 1924, Book IV. The section in Chapter III of that book, dealing with 'The ordinary course of a fluctuation of commercial credit' has the following footnote attached to its heading: 'Much of this Section is reproduced from *Economics of Industry* by the present writer and his wife, published in 1879.'

6.　Marshall 1899.

7.　Lawlor 1994, p. 207.

8.　Emery 1896, pp. 109 and 112.

9.　Ibid., p. 184.

10.　Lavington 1921, pp. 248–249.

11.　Keynes 1913.

12.　Keynes 1912.

13.　Keynes 1930, Book IV.

14.　Ibid., Volume I, pp. 202–205.

15.　See above, pp. 43–45 and Keynes 1930, Volume I, pp. 194–195.

16.　Keynes 1930, Volume II, Chapter 37.

17.　Ibid., p. 355.

18.　Ibid., p. 358.

19.　It was only in 1938 that Hawtrey published *A Century of Bank Rate* in which he showed clearly that, over the century in which Bank Rate had been operational, bond rates had been more stable than money market rates. The implied anchoring of the long end of the yield curve was then absorbed into the financial economics of Michał Kalecki. See below, Chapter 11.

20.　Keynes 1930, Volume II, pp. 357–361.

21.　Lavington 1921.

22.　Kahn 1972.

23.　Keynes 1930, Volume II, pp. 364 and 368.

24.　Ibid., p. 361. 'The rate of interest … is not causally determined by the value set by the conditions of supply and demand for new loans at the margin. Rather are the demand and supply schedules for new loans determined by the value set by the market on existing loans (of similar types).' Townshend 1937.

25.　Keynes 1930, Volume II, p. 371.

26.　Ibid., p. 373.

27.　Keynes 1931b, p. 349.

28.　Ibid., p. 350.

29.　Ibid., p. 353.

30.　Ibid., p. 354.

31.　Ibid., p. 365.

32.　Ibid.

33.　Schumpeter noted that deposits rose in the London clearing banks, and banks abroad, but 'to the last quarter of 1935, advances contributed next to nothing to this expansion of deposits' (Schumpeter 1939, p. 959). Susan Howson pointed out that new capital issues in the British capital market remained very low in the case of imperial and foreign issues, but domestic issues recovered until 1936, when they fell off again. Howson 1975, pp. 104–106.

34.　Keynes 1933a, p. 434.

35.　Ibid., p. 435.

36.　Keynes 1931a, p. 424.

7. John Maynard Keynes's financial theory of under-investment: towards uncertainty

In the *General Theory* Keynes abandoned the view expounded in the *Treatise on Money* of the capitalist economy made unstable by credit cycles and re-cast his analysis as an explanation of under-employment *equilibrium*, reflecting the stagnationist trend in the capitalist economies during the 1930s. This emphasis on equilibrium was to challenge those economists who expected an imminent return to full employment. But it also placed an ambiguity at the heart of his work inviting, on the one hand, a search for the market 'rigidity' ('sticky real wages') that was preventing the realisation of a full employment equilibrium, while retaining, on the other hand, the elements of his critique of a capitalism made wayward by its financial system.[1] The *General Theory* also contains, alongside the analysis of an under-employment equilibrium created by the *financial* system described below, a theory of a capitalist economy brought to under-employment by its use of money. This latter theory became the staple of later Keynesian explanations of economic disturbance and stagnation. Expounding a *monetary* theory of economic disturbance in the context of a financial one increased the scope for the interpretive ambiguity that has dogged Keynes's economic thought.

On his way to a more generalised theory that would incorporate factors capable of producing the 'abnormal' under-investment not amenable to financial or monetary policy, Keynes advanced a theory of 'own' rates of interest. This is distinctive in being particular to the *General Theory*, although Keynes refers to Sraffa as having originated it.[2] It advanced a *monetary* explanation of under-employment, as opposed to the *financial* theory of under-investment *in the face of uncertainty* with which he ended the *General Theory*.

7.1   FROM OWN RATES OF INTEREST TO SPECULATION

The theory of 'own rates of interest' was drafted at the end of 1934, when it formed Chapter 19 of the first draft of the *General Theory*. The first title of that chapter, 'Philosophical Considerations on the Essential Properties of Capital, Interest and Money', reveals Keynes's attempt to step back from his policy focus on a transmission mechanism from the financial markets to company investment, to take in more general characteristics of economic activity. The chapter eventually appeared as Chapter 17 in the published book with its title 'The Essential Properties of Interest and Money' unchanged from the first draft. In an attempt to escape capital productivity theories of interest, an essential feature of the 'classical' economics which he now sought to overturn, Keynes put forward the idea that all commodities may be deemed to have their 'own' rate of interest. This is the net benefit from holding them over time. Keynes argued that this net benefit consists of the yield or net output of the commodity (income and appreciation in money terms), minus its carrying cost (cost of storage), plus its liquidity premium (the 'power of disposal over an asset'). Included in this was also supposed to be a 'risk premium', i.e. the holder's 'confidence' in the expected yield of the commodity. Because money cannot be easily produced (it 'has both in the long and in the short period, a zero, or at any rate a very small, elasticity of production'), and has a negligible elasticity of substitution, its own rate of interest, the money rate of interest, is the standard against which other own rates are measured. If the own rates of other reproducible commodities are higher, more of those commodities will be produced for gain, gradually reducing their 'own' rate of return until there is no advantage in production, as opposed to holding money:

> Thus, with other commodities left to themselves, 'natural forces', i.e., the ordinary forces of the market, would tend to bring their rate of interest down until the emergence of full employment has brought about for commodities generally the inelasticity of supply which we have postulated as a normal characteristic of money. Thus, in the absence of money and – we must also suppose – of any other commodity with the assumed characteristics of money, the rates of interest would only reach equilibrium when there is full employment.[3]

This analysis gave rise to long discussions with Hawtrey and Robertson over the meaning and significance of 'own' rates of interest. Keynes eventually concluded:

> I admit the obscurity of this chapter. A time may come when I am, so to speak, sufficiently familiar with my own ideas to make it easier. But at present I doubt if the chapter is any use, except to someone who has entered into, and is sympathetic with, the ideas in the previous chapters; to which it has, I think, to be regarded as posterior. For it is far easier to argue the ideas involved in the much simpler way in which they arise in the chapter on liquidity preference.[4]

However, even Keynes's partisans have been considerably more critical of the chapter. Alvin Hansen described it as 'a detour which could be omitted without sacrificing the main argument'.[5] More recently, Fiona MacLachlan has written that it 'is undoubtedly muddled and it appears that Keynes was grasping at ideas that he had not successfully sorted through in his own mind'.[6]

It was Hicks who put his finger on the essential inconsistency in Keynes's analysis in this part of the *General Theory*. There is no evidence that he had been involved in Keynes's discussions on this chapter when they were being drafted, although the parallels with Hicks's own thinking are apparent, and Hicks was lecturing in Cambridge from 1935 to 1938. They corresponded afterwards, but the correspondence was quickly taken up with the interpretation that Hicks put forward of the *General Theory* in his seminal article 'Mr. Keynes and the Classics'. However, their correspondence started with Hicks's review of the *General Theory*. In particular, their earlier letters focused on Keynes's Liquidity Preference theory of money. At one point, Hicks wrote up his criticisms, of which the bulk was a section headed 'The own rates of interest'. Here he concluded:

> After a great deal of thought, I have become convinced that the argument of your Chapter 17 gets tied up because you do not distinguish sufficiently between investment that does employ labour and investment that does not. If the monetary system is inelastic, a mere increase in the desire to hold stocks of coffee, which itself does nothing directly for employment, may raise the rate of interest, and thus actually diminish employment on balance – at least apart from the effect on anticipations, and hence on the production of coffee. Similarly, in a coffee world, a rise in the desire to hold stocks of money will raise the coffee rate of interest (if the supply of coffee is imperfectly elastic) and this will similarly tend to lessen employment.[7]

Hicks was evidently here trying to recover the stable relationship between the rate of interest and investment that was a feature of his exposition in 'Mr. Keynes and the Classics', a draft of which Hicks enclosed with his letter to Keynes. But it is nevertheless a curious intervention, because Hicks himself had earlier sketched out some of the ideas that Keynes was to put into his *General Theory* in a paper which Hicks read at the London Economic Club in 1934. This appeared the following February in *Economica* as 'A Suggestion for Simplifying the Theory of Money'. The paper is today known mainly as one of the first expositions of a 'portfolio' theory of money. Here he presented 'a sort of generalized balance-sheet, suitable for all individuals and institutions'. This had on the assets side the whole range of commodities available in a modern capitalist economy, including perishable and durable consumption goods, money, bank deposits, short- and long-term debts, stocks and shares and 'productive equipment (including goods in process)'.[8] Eshag later indicated that 'the relationship between the rate of earnings on different categories of assets and their degree of marketability' could be traced back to Lavington, Thornton and Giffen.[9]

Nicholas Kaldor may arguably have made the best sense out of the chapter in his 1939 paper on 'Speculation and Economic Activity'. Kaldor's paper sought to make Keynes's theory of 'own rates of interest' consistent with not only the Liquidity Preference theory of money, presented in chapters 13 and 14 of the *General Theory*, but also Keynes's analysis of speculation in Chapter 12 of that work. Kaldor argued that 'if Keynes had made the theory of the own rate of interest, suitably expanded, the centre-piece of his exposition in the *General Theory*, a great deal of the subsequent interest controversy might have been avoided'.[10] In his view the theory was an explanation of speculative behaviour. However:

> In the real world there are only two classes of assets which satisfy the conditions necessary for large-scale speculation. The first consists of certain raw materials, dealt in at organised produce exchanges. The second consists of standardised future claims to property, i.e. bonds and shares. It is obvious that the suitability of the second class for speculative purposes is much greater than that of the first. Bonds and shares are perfect objects for speculation; they possess all the necessary attributes to a maximum degree. They are perfectly standardised (one particular share of a company is just as good as any other); perfectly durable (if the paper they are written on goes bad its can be easily replaced); their value is very high in proportion to bulk (storage cost is zero or a nominal amount); and in addition they (normally) have a yield, which is invariant (in the short period at any rate) with respect to the size of the specu-

lative commitments. Hence their net carrying cost can never be positive, and in the majority of cases is negative.[11]

George Shackle and Victoria Chick have drawn attention to a complementary interpretation, which was advanced by Hugh Townshend, a former student of Keynes's, in response to a review article by Hicks on the *General Theory*. Townshend argued that the rate of interest is not determined by conditions of supply and demand in some notional market for new loans, as Hicks's loanable funds interpretation of the *General Theory* suggested, but in the market for existing loans. There, as Keynes had argued, values are essentially conventional: 'the influence of expectations about the value of existing loans is usually the preponderating causal factor in determining the common price'.[12] Since the values of longer-term securities can change overnight, no equilibrium between the supply of funds and the demand for new loans is possible. Accordingly, both Shackle and Chick have put forward Townshend's view as a methodological critique of general equilibrium interpretations, rather than as a theory of financial disturbance.[13]

In Chapter 12 of the *General Theory* Keynes made a fundamental distinction between the purchase of securities for resale at a higher price, which he termed speculation, and enterprise, buying securities for long-term income. He lamented the predominance of speculation over enterprise, which he believed reduced companies' productive investment in plant, machinery and technology to incidental outcomes of a 'casino', mere 'bubbles on the whirlpool of speculation'. But he concluded that there is no other effective way of providing additional finance for investment.[14]

In that same chapter, Keynes put forward his theory of stock prices, the famous beauty contest, in which speculators buy and sell stocks according to how they believe that the other speculators or participants in the market will on average evaluate those stocks in the future:

Professional investment may be likened to those newspaper competitions in which the competitors have to pick out the six prettiest faces from a hundred photographs, the prize being awarded to the competitor whose choice most nearly corresponds to the average preferences of the competitors as a whole; so that each competitor has to pick, not those faces which he himself finds prettiest, but those which he thinks likeliest to catch the fancy of the other competitors, all of whom are looking at the problem from the same point of view. It is not a case of choosing those which, to the best of one's judgement, are really the prettiest, nor even those which average opinion genuinely thinks the prettiest. We have reached the third degree where we devote our intelligences to anticipating what average opinion expects the average opinion to be. And there are some, I believe, who practise the fourth, fifth and higher degrees.[15]

Market evaluations are a '*convention* ... that the existing state of affairs will continue indefinitely, except in so far as we have specific reasons to expect a change'.[16] It is impossible to resist 'average opinion' in favour of more rational, long-term considerations: 'For it is not sensible to pay 25 for an investment of which you believe the prospective yield to justify a value of 30, if you also believe that the market will value it at 20 three months hence.'[17]

7.2   CONCENTRATING ON UNCERTAINTY

The reason for this dependence on subjective evaluations and their coagulation into conventional market values is uncertainty. Like the entrepreneur deciding whether to install new equipment, the speculator cannot know the future value of his investment. He can only make judgements with a greater or lesser degree of 'confidence' according to the 'weight' of the evidence he has available to him. Accordingly, speculators' 'confidence' veers between optimism and pessimism. Furthermore, expectations in their turn are determined more by recent experience than by the more distant past.[18] Such confidence therefore tends to become over-optimistic as a boom matures, and over-pessimistic as a recession is prolonged.

Uncertainty about the future is the key to understanding the adherence of traders to conventions and past experience. It also explains an apparent inconsistency that arises in Keynes's 'Notes on the Trade Cycle' in the *General Theory*, where he expounded his view of an expectations-driven business cycle. He argued that 'a serious fall in the marginal efficiency of capital also tends to affect adversely the propensity to consume ...' through 'a severe decline in the market value of Stock Exchange equities'. The marginal efficiency of capital was defined by Keynes in subjective terms as 'the *expectation* of yield' in relation to 'the *current* supply price of the capital-asset'.[19] He then proceeded to argue that changes in securities' prices affect the consumption of rentiers, 'the class who take an active interest in their Stock Exchange investments'. The fall in consumption 'serves to aggravate still further the depressing effect of a decline in the marginal efficiency of capital'. No mention is made here of Keynes's earlier justification of the stock market as a source of finance for business investment, and its implication that such finance would be less readily available, and certainly more expensive, if stock prices are falling. Hence Shackle's later opinion that Chapter 12 may 'appear at first reading as a strange intruder into the main current of thought' of the *General Theory*. Shackle believed that opinion on the stock market may be less self-regarding, and more symptomatic of general business confidence.[20] Later, in response to criticism of his monetary analysis from Bertil Ohlin, Keynes stated that entrepreneurs who cannot finance investments out of their own savings do so by borrowing from banks. This then became an additional, 'finance', motive for augmenting the demand for money.[21] In this view, business investment depends more on the rate of interest than on stock market prices.

Keynes's theory of the speculative demand for money may have given him the clue as to how finance may lead to a permanent regime of under-investment. The speculative demand for liquidity, as Keynes called it, was the money held by traders in the securities markets awaiting profitable investment opportunities in those markets. As Keynes put it, it has 'the object of securing profit from knowing better than the market what the future will bring forth'.[22] In this respect it is a counter-tendency to the conventions established by the 'beauty contest' in the stock market. Only if the speculative demand for money is held in check would increases in the supply of money reduce the rate of interest.[23] But even this may not be enough to overcome business uncertainty about the prospective yield on investments. Once this yield falls, then even a low interest rate may be insufficient to stimulate investment: 'a high rate of interest is much more effective against a boom than a low rate of interest against a slump'.[24] Keynes thus identified the limits to the manipulation of economic growth by monetary policy. This lay in the volatility of the prospective yield on investments:

> Thus the remedy for the boom is not a higher rate of interest but a lower rate of interest. For that may enable the so-called boom to last. The right remedy for the trade cycle is not to be found in abolishing booms and thus keeping us permanently in a semi-slump, but in abolishing slumps and thus keeping us permanently in a quasi-boom ...
> The boom which is destined to end in a slump is caused, therefore, by the combination of a rate of interest, which in a correct state of expectation would be too high for full employment, with a misguided state of expectation which, so long as it lasts, prevents this rate of interest from being in fact deterrent.

A boom is a situation in which over-optimism triumphs over a rate of interest which, in a cooler light, would be seen to be excessive.[25]

Hence, in contrast to his resignation in the face of 'speculation' in Chapter 12, Keynes concluded his analysis by urging the 'euthanasia of the rentier' and the socialisation of investment.[26] This was because of the dependence of capitalist investment on the conjuncture in the financial markets. This dependence on finance put expectations of yield at the forefront of investment considerations. It required the lowering of the rate of interest to raise investment to the point where full employment was achieved:

> The scale of investment is promoted by a *low* rate of interest, provided that we do not attempt to stimulate it in this way beyond the point which corresponds to full employment. Thus it is to our best advantage to reduce the rate of interest to that point relatively to the schedule of the marginal efficiency of capital at which there is full employment.[27]

In the long run, however, this dependence of investment on finance was already in the process of being overcome: 'the euthanasia of the rentier, of the functionless investor, will be nothing sudden, merely a gradual but prolonged continuance of what we have seen recently in Great Britain, and will need no revolution'.[28]

Keynes reiterated this explanation of under-investment a short time later in his paper 'The General Theory of Employment'. The socialisation of investment was essential because, in the course of the 1930s, Keynes had come to doubt that it was possible to maintain adequate levels of investment by fixing the conjuncture in the financial markets. This was because of the nature of the investment decision in the face of ignorance of the future, i.e. uncertainty.[29]

Thus, the *General Theory* was not only Keynes's considered view on how the economy worked as a whole, and hence the book may be viewed as a cross-section of the ideas which he had in his mind in the mid-1930s. It was also a critique of the way in which long-term securities markets finance companies. But, above all, one can argue, the *General Theory* is a response to the failure of monetary policy to influence those markets in such a way as to allow them to do more effectively what the conventional wisdom of his time and ours tells us that they do superlatively, namely finance investment. Although 'Keynesian' policy is now universally associated with aggregate demand management through fiscal policy, in fact in his book Keynes only mentioned fiscal policy in passing as an influence on the marginal propensity to consume.[30] His preferred fiscal stimulus was through public works. His essential message, which he later declared to be his original contribution in the *General Theory* was the introduction of uncertainty and expectations as factors preventing the long-term rate of interest from falling to stimulate investment up to its full employment level.[31]

In his 'Notes on the Trade Cycle', Chapter 22 of the *General Theory*, Keynes appeared to turn away from a financial explanation of economic disturbance:

> We have been accustomed in explaining the 'crisis' to lay stress on the rising tendency of the rate of interest under the influence of the increased demand for money both for trade and speculative purposes. At times this factor may certainly play an aggravating and, occasionally perhaps, an initiating part. But I suggest that a more typical, and often the predominant, explanation of the crisis is, not primarily a rise in the rate of interest, but a sudden collapse in the marginal efficiency of capital ... Liquidity-preference, except those manifestations of it which are associated with increasing trade and speculation, does not increase until *after* the collapse in the marginal efficiency of capital.[32]

Keynes went on to argue that movements in the stock market had a more pronounced 'wealth' effect on consumption:

> Unfortunately a serious fall in the marginal efficiency of capital also tends to affect adversely the propensity to consume ... With a 'stock-minded' public, as in the United States today, a rising stock market may be an almost essential condition of a satisfactory propensity to consume; and this circumstance, generally overlooked until lately, obviously serves to aggravate still further the depressing effect of a decline in the marginal efficiency of capital.[33]

Keynes then concluded by arguing that the financial markets tend to concentrate, rather than disperse, volatile expectations of returns from investments with a longer time horizon than the markets have. This is aggravated by the effect of changes in stock market values on consumption:

> Thus, with markets organised and influenced as they are at present, the market estimation of the marginal efficiency of capital may suffer such enormously wide fluctuations that it cannot be sufficiently off-set by corresponding fluctuations in the rate of interest. Moreover, the corresponding movements in the stock market may, as we have seen above, depress the propensity to consume just when it is most needed. In conditions of *laissez-faire* the avoidance of wide fluctuations in employment may, therefore, prove impossible without

a far-reaching change in the psychology of investment market such as there is no reason to expect. I conclude that the duty of ordering the current volume of investment cannot safely be left in private hands.[34]

In the *General Theory* and beyond, Keynes made use of two explanations of under-investment. One was a financial theory of under-investment, due to excessive long-term interest rates. This fits in neatly with his consistent advocacy, from the *Treatise* onwards, of open market operations to bring down the long-term rate of interest in order to stimulate investment.[35] The other lay in the nature of investment, which requires the capitalist entrepreneur to take a view on an uncertain future. When the experience of the 1930s revealed the difficulties of guiding investment through monetary policy, Keynes put forward uncertainty in the process of investment decision-making as an additional explanatory variable. As Susan Howson and Donald Winch put it:

> [In 1936], Keynes's major policy goal was still the stability of the economy at a high level of employment; but the perspective on the instruments and the difficulties of achieving this goal reflected five years of thought plus the experience of the slump. Given that investment was the motive force of the system, employment policy had to regulate investment. An appropriate monetary policy directed at long-term interest rates, as in the *Treatise* would provide the right long-term environment. In contrast to the *Treatise*, however, where monetary policy was expected to do *all* the work, it might not, given the state of entrepreneurial expectations, provide the solution to short-term instabilities. For that fiscal regulation might be necessary, particularly if the monetary authorities found it inexpedient to operate in long-term securities markets rather than relying on Bank rate. Open market purchases of Treasury bills or other short-term securities could only affect long rates indirectly, and it was long-term rates – very much subject 'the state of news' – that affected the bulk of investment.[36]

7.3 LIMITS OF INTEREST RATE POLICY

To the end of his life, Keynes held to the view that the rate of interest was crucial for investment, but that its influence was modified at low levels. As late as 1945, in his 'Notes for the National Debt Enquiry', Keynes wrote: 'The rate of interest ... is one of the influences affecting the inducement to invest. Experience shows, however, that whilst a high rate of interest is capable of having a dominating influence on inducement to invest, it becomes relatively unimportant at low levels, compared with the expectations affecting the inducement.'[37] As part of a fiscal regime to maintain a high level of investment, Keynes recommended keeping down the long-term rate of interest by open market operations with a permanent tap issue.[38]

Keynes's profound insights, as well as his inconsistencies, ensured that subsequent discussion of the relationship of finance to the real economy took place in the shadow of his analysis. There is no inconsistency between a strictly financial theory of under-investment, and a more essentialist uncertainty theory of under-investment. But Keynes's more philosophical followers, notably George Shackle, have tended to empha-sise the principles of uncertainty in his theory. Keynes's more financially rooted followers and critics, the remnants of the Swedish School and Minsky, have tended to emphasise the limits imposed on investment by the financial markets.

Minsky in particular criticised Keynes for his failure to include 'the price of capital assets in his statement of the liquidity-preference function' and hence stating his argument solely in terms of the rate of interest.[39] This was to be remedied by Keynes's perhaps most thoughtful colleague and advocate, Joan Robinson. In *The Accumulation of Capital* she postulates that, with bonds assumed to be irredeemable to remove the effects of different terms to maturity, their yield is differentiated accord-ing to the perceived risk of default of the issuer. When confidence is high, the spread around the current money market rate of interest is reduced:

> The yield of a bond at any moment reflects both the general level of interest rates and the particular credit of the particular concerns (those most respected and reliable enjoying the lowest yields). We may select the very best concerns about whose ability to honour their obligations there is the least possible doubt, as a marker, and call the yield of their bonds *the* bond rate of interest. Others have higher yields in varying degrees. The relative yields fan out in times of insecurity and lie close together in periods of general prosperity when profits are easy to earn and fears of default are far from everyone's thoughts.[40]

The implied yield curve is flat during an economic boom and acquires a positive slope during a recession. However, there is a notable absence of any influence of Keynesian 'liquidity preference' which would lead one to suppose that longer-term stocks would pay a margin over the short-term rate of interest as a 'liquidity premium' against the possibility of illiquidity.

Further on, Robinson attributes high bond rates to active interest rate policy by the monetary authorities:

> Generally speaking, the wider and less predictable are fluctuations in the level of interest rates, the higher, on the average, the level will tend to be, for it is uncertainty about future interest rates which gives rise to a reluctance to hold bonds and keeps up their yields ... Thus we must add to the list of causes of stagnation to which capitalist economies are subject, stagnation due to a chronic tendency for interest rates to rule too high, relatively to the rate of profit, to permit accumulation to go on.

At this point a footnote is added 'This is one of the main contentions of Keynes's *General Theory*.'[41]

Eprime Eshag's pioneering research at the end of the 1950s, reiterated recently by David Laidler, confirms that 'there was nothing of great significance which could be regarded as wholly original in Keynes's formal analysis of the rate of interest. What he did, in effect, was to develop and elucidate the ideas known at Cambridge prior to the appearance of the *General Theory* in 1936.'[42] In particular:

> The excessive importance attached by Keynes to changes in the quantity of money and in the rate of interest in determining the volume of investment has been distinctly harmful in practice. The general impression given by Keynes's work on the rate of interest is that changes in the rate of interest, which in practice range from a fraction of 1 per cent to 1 or 2 per cent at a time, can produce a very significant *direct* impact on the volume of investment and on the level of economic activity. The prevalence of the notion that the level of investment and income can be significantly influenced by changes in the rate of interest within the range mentioned above, accompanied by corresponding variations in the quantity of money, which is found not only among the orthodox economists and bankers, but also among some leading Keynesian economists, can be traced, in the case of the latter group, partly at least, to the influence of Keynes ... In this respect, Keynes was still operating under the influence of the classical economists and Marshall.[43]

Eshag here revealed the influence on him of Kalecki. In fact there was more to Keynes's analysis of capitalism than just the theory of money and an almost classical theory of investment. Keynes's analysis of money and investment in the context of a capitalist economy dominated by finance produced a financial theory of under-investment to explain the decline into economic depression at the start of the 1930s. In his final years, as he tackled the problem of government indebtedness, Keynes became even more aware of this financial aspect.[44] For a while he believed this to be amenable to treatment by expansionary monetary policy. With the failure of this policy in the 1930s, he shifted the grounds of his critique to the way in which finance makes investment depend on uncertainty and expectations, as well as the rate of interest.

NOTES

1. This is further discussed in Chick 1996.
2. Keynes 1936, p. 223. According to Fiona MacLachlan Keynes 'borrowed' the idea from Piero Sraffa (MacLachlan 1993, p. 97).
3. Keynes 1936, p. 235.
4. Ibid., p. 519.
5. Hansen 1953, p. 155.
6. MacLachlan 1993, pp. 96–97.
7. Keynes 1973b, pp. 78–79.
8. Hicks 1935, pp. 74–75.
9. Eshag 1963, pp. 65–66.
10. Kaldor 1960, p. 6.
11. Kaldor 1939, pp. 22–23.
12. Townshend 1937.
13. Shackle 1967, pp. 246–248; Chick 1987.
14. In this regard too, Lavington turns out to have been considerably more critical. In *The English Capital Market*, Lavington concluded that 'the amount of capital annually passing through the securities market and applied to the extension of the business equipment of the country is comparatively small, and is probably in the neighbourhood of one quarter of the whole'. The main contribution of the securities market to business was providing liquidity rather than capital (Lavington 1921, pp. 280–281).
15. Keynes 1936, p. 156.
16. Ibid., p. 152.
17. Ibid., p. 156.
18. '... the present is a much more serviceable guide to the future than a candid examination of past experience would show it to have been hitherto' (Keynes 1937a, p. 114).
19. Keynes 1936, p. 136.
20. Shackle 1967, pp. 132–133.
21. Keynes 1937b; see also Chick 1983, pp. 198–200.
22. Keynes 1936, p. 170.
23. Ibid., p. 171.
24. Ibid., p. 320.
25. Ibid., p. 322.
26. Ibid., pp. 375–377. With an error that is perhaps more acute than the correct original, Hobson welcomed Keynes's conversion to critical finance as follows: 'His theory of interest enables him to foresee the way of getting rid of the scarcity of capital and the income paid for its use. He predicts the "enthusiasm of the *rentier*, the functionless investor," and assigns to the

State the "socialization of investment" as "the only means of securing an approximation to full employment."' Hobson 1938b, p. 213.

27. Keynes 1936, p. 375.
28. Ibid., p. 376.
29. Keynes 1937a; Shackle 1967, p. 136.
30. Keynes 1936, pp. 94–95.
31. Keynes 1937a.
32. Keynes 1936, pp. 315–316, emphasis in the original.
33. Ibid., p. 319.
34. Ibid., p. 320.
35. Keynes 1930, Volume II, pp. 371–373; Keynes 1936, p. 206.
36. Howson and Winch 1977, pp. 138–139.
37. Keynes 1945, p. 390.
38. Ibid. A tap issue is a bond issue that is sold into the market as required over an extended period of time, rather than on a particular issue day.
39. Minsky 1975, pp. 69–70.
40. Robinson 1956, p. 230.
41. Ibid., p. 242. In her essay 'The Rate of Interest' (Robinson 1952, p. 6) Joan Robinson wrote that 'uncertainty of future capital value ... due not to any fear of failure by the borrower but to the possibility of changes in capital values owing to changes in the ruling rate of interest ... is the main ingredient in Keynes's concept of liquidity preference. He regards the rate of interest primarily as a premium against the possible loss of capital if an asset has to be realised before its redemption date.'
42. Eshag 1963, p. 66; Laidler 1999.
43. Eshag 1963, p. 68.
44. Tily 2007, see especially Chapter 7.

PART III

Critical theories of finance in the twentieth century: corporate debt and crisis

8.   The principle of increasing risk: Marek Breit

As Keynes was developing his financial theory of under-investment, new ideas were emerging elsewhere in Europe, in more direct reaction to German monetary theory and Wicksell. The key figures here were Marek Breit (1907–1942), Michał Kalecki (1899–1970) and Josef Steindl (1912–1993). Their working lives spanned the middle decades of the twentieth century, from the 1930s up to the 1980s. Marek Breit was a Polish economist, too briefly active in his profession during the 1930s, who was tragically killed during the German occupation of his country. Josef Steindl, an Austrian economist, worked in Britain during the Second World War, and continued to write until 1990. They had in common the experience of working with the Polish economist Michał Kalecki, and their shared commitment to what the latter enunciated as the Principle of Increasing Risk.

8.1   FROM FREE BANKING

The idea behind the Principle originates in the work of Marek Breit. He came from a Jewish background in Kraków, and studied at the Jagiellonian University in his home town. His only book, *Stopa Procentowa w Polsce* (The Rate of Interest in Poland) published in Kraków in 1933, has all the appearance of a doctoral thesis. Given his background, Breit could hardly have aspired to appointment in Poland's notoriously conservative universities. In the year of the book's publication he moved to Warsaw where Edward Lipiński later recruited him to the Institute for Research in Business Cycles and Prices (Instytut Badania Konjunktur Gospodarczych i Cen). Kalecki was already working at the Institute. Breit's main task was writing reports on credit markets in Poland. But the development of his ideas at this time clearly shows the influence of Kalecki's monetary and business cycle theories. In 1936, Breit and the third outstanding economist at the Institute, Ludwik Landau, openly criticised the deflationary policies of the Polish Finance Minister, Eugeniusz

Kwiatkowski, under whose patronage the Institute had been established. Kwiatkowski demanded their removal, and the two were sacked. Lacking the international connections that brought Kalecki (and Oskar Lange) out of Poland on Rockefeller Foundation Fellowships, Breit remained in Poland and was killed in 1942.

In the English language economics literature, an important essay by Alberto Chilosi[1] is the only extant discussion of Breit's monetary analysis. In Breit's own country, Tadeusz Kowalik's erudite history of modern Polish economics[2] discusses Breit, but the bulk of the discussion is devoted to the financial model of the socialist economy which he wrote with Oskar Lange in 1934.[3] In personal discussion, Kowalik reported Kalecki's view that Breit's early work was neo-classical. It was certainly influenced by Austrian monetary theory. In his maturity Kalecki would have objected to Breit's *classical* conviction that the rate of interest influences the volume of investment. Kowalik has also written that Breit was influenced by Wicksell.[4] Breit was indeed neo-classical in Keynes' meaning of the term, in that he did not consider actual saving and investment to be equal. In the more common sense of someone who adheres to laissez-faire and marginalist doctrines, Breit's book was certainly neo-classical. But the conclusion of his only paper published outside Poland, in German in 1935 as 'Ein Beitrag zur Theorie des Geld-und Kapitalmarktes' in the *Zeitschrift für Nationalökonomie*, contains intriguing hints at Kalecki's later scepticism about the influence that conditions of credit may have on investment. Common to all his work is a clearly Schumpeterian monetary analysis and view of capitalist production as a process rather than a series of discrete production decisions. In his book, Breit went even further and subjected Wicksell and Schumpeter to a more profound critique, and he eventually rejected their business cycle views, implicitly if not explicitly. The originality of this thinker and the obscurity of his work, in a world increasingly dominated by English language discussion, warrant a more extensive examination of his analysis.

Although published in 1933, *Stopa Procentowa w Polsce* was in fact written in 1930. This is important, because it reveals the source of Breit's preoccupation in the book with inflation. During the first half of the 1920s, Poland had experienced hyperinflation, which was finally brought to an end by the Grabski reforms of 1926, which introduced a new currency linked to the US dollar. By the time the book was published, Poland was in the severe economic depression that brought financial deflation to the forefront of Breit's preoccupations in the articles that he published after 1933.

The book commences in orthodox Austrian fashion, arguing that the rate of interest establishes a natural equilibrium between saving and the amount of resources which society wishes to devote to the establishment of more productive 'roundabout' methods of production (the Austrian theory of capital). Breit argued that this equilibrium is prevented by government intervention, 'étatism', which distorted this equilibrium in three ways. First of all, the government engaged directly in unprofitable ventures. Second, government banks in Poland supported private enterprise with cheap credit. Third, the government imposed interest rate ceilings below the equilibrium rate of interest. However, governments can only effectively reduce short-term rates of interest, because long-term rates are determined in the credit markets. This creates a further disparity between short-term rates of interest and the long-term rate of interest.[5] All this was of course common ground to Austrian critics of government monetary intervention, such as Hayek, as well as recent financial liberalisers. It undoubtedly explains why Kalecki reacted so unfavourably to the new arrival from Kraków at the Institute.

Breit's critique of government intervention in the credit market, which would otherwise naturally bring about an equilibrium between saving and investment in the economy,[6] indicates Breit's inclination, at least at the time when he was writing the book, towards a 'general equilibrium' view of finance. In fact, his monetary analysis reveals the means by which the banking and financial system may itself disturb the economy. Among these are centrally allocated credit quotas and interest ceilings. These, he argued, are responsible for the misallocation of credit in the economy, leading to inefficient investment in the economy.[7] This is well known today from the work of Hayek and financial liberalisers such as Ronald MacKinnon and Maxwell Fry. In a paragraph that would have complemented rather well Hawtrey's analysis, of which he seems to have been unaware, Breit pointed out that credit rationing and interest ceilings (Poland had reintroduced a usury law in June 1924) led to fluctuations in the reserves of smaller private banks on the fringes of the banking system. This is because they were unable to reduce the demand for credit by raising the rate of interest, and were therefore obliged to ration credit. Such rationing, in turn caused shifts in the prudence with which these banks viewed the investment projects of entrepreneurs. When banks had strong reserves they tended to be careless about lending out money. When they had weaker reserves, banks tended to be over-cautious about their lending.[8] Hence, and in contrast to Adam Smith's view, Breit associated low rates of interest with poorer quality loans. The artificial scarcity of loans at such rates discouraged their repayment.[9]

Along with Hayek and recent financial liberalisers, Breit emphasised that state control of credit created monopolistic distortions. The intervention of the state in interest rate policy and through its ownership of large banks in Poland at the time brought about an excess demand for credit and disintermediation of savings from the formal banking system.[10] At the end of his book, he put forward a credit cycle model that, in its essentials, is the same as the one that Hayek put forward a short time afterwards in London.[11] This credit cycle need not detain the discussion here, since it is driven not by the autonomous functioning of the financial system, but by 'misconceived' state direction of credit or interest rates. However, Breit took this analysis much further than more recent critics of state intervention in banking, and made it into the foundation of his monetary theory.

Breit divided the money supply into two parts. The first of these was the 'money supply arising from the normal circulation of the static economy', and the second was 'additional money supply whose sources lie in the dynamic shifts of the modern money-credit economy'. This additional money supply is also called 'inflationary credit'.[12] The first, consisting of 'normal means of payment', is clearly a notion drawn from Schumpeter's analysis of money in his *Theory of Economic Development*, as also is Breit's terminology for describing capitalist activity as making 'combinations' of factors of production.[13] The second category of money supply, inflationary credit, was also common currency in the German monetary theory that was the foundation of his analysis.[14] The whole of chapter three in his book is devoted to the explanation of inflationary credit.

Inflationary credit is credit to which no additional commodity production corresponds, although it may exist in the future if additional production is undertaken with it. According to Breit, it arises because of the monopolistic power of banks. This monopoly power allows them to issue additional credit without loss of their reserves. The most obvious monopoly is that of central banks, which are given a formal monopoly of rights of bank-note issue by governments.[15] This additional money supply brings the money rate of interest below its 'natural' level. Breit criticised Schumpeter and Wicksell for seeing the source of that money rate of interest in the supply of and demand for money in the wholesale money markets, whereas its true origins lie in the international bank cartel that accepts into its members' reserves the additional means of payment that they issue.[16] Thus Breit attributed credit disturbances not only to inappropriate monetary and credit policies by the government, but also to an absence of competition among banks, that would limit their inflationary credit creation.[17]

Breit at this time was clearly close to a view known as 'free banking'.[18] Its most articulate spokesmen, such as Henry Meulen, who was active during the first four decades of the century, and more recently Hayek, argued that banks naturally evolved towards an ideal system that limited credit creation to non-inflationary dimensions.[19] Breit did not mention any of this literature, nor is it discussed by the authors he cited: Böhm-Bawerk, Cassel, Hahn, Kock, Mises, Spiethoff, Wicksell and Schumpeter. The 'free banking' school attributed monetary disorders to the appropriation by the state and its agencies of control over credit creation.[20] Breit, however, stands out from the 'free banking' school. He saw that bank cartels could arise among banks in the same way that they arose among other commercial concerns, even just through the operations of the inter-bank market:

> It is generally known that within states, banks creating accounts have for a long time combined in cartels, setting their conditions of credit on the same basis ('Konditionenkartell').

This inflationary credit expansion exposes central banks to the possibility of falling foreign currency reserves. Accordingly, central banks join in an international cartel to maintain stable exchange rates:

> This involves the co-operation of the whole credit-creation system on a world scale … With such a wide monopoly, there are no external obstacles to the inflationary moves of the world-wide bank cartel.[21]

In fact this cooperation by banks is an essential feature of their management of their liquidity and asset quality.[22] Breit's exposition of the inflationary implications of such cooperation is a more profound dilemma of institutional design than he may have realised.

8.2   PERCEPTIONS OF RISK

By the time that Breit's inflationary fears had been put into print, the financial situation he was observing had changed dramatically. The Polish economy was beset by depression. Like other 'producers', the

Institute where he came to work cut the prices of its publications in an effort to promote their sale. As a result of expansionary monetary policy by the central bank the Polish banking system was able to maintain its liquidity. In his book, Breit had argued that the long-term loans market comes into operation once the short-term loans market is 'satiated'.[23] But the extension of the long-term loan market in Poland and elsewhere at this time was distress lending rather than the financing of new investment opportunities. Short-term loans could not be repaid and banks were forced to roll them over, if they were not to admit them as bad loans, while the state banks were obliged to extend long-term loans to business to prevent industrial collapse.[24]

At the Institute for Research in Business Cycles and Prices Michał Kalecki introduced Breit to the new principles of aggregate demand that were to make German monetary theory obsolete in the 1930s. A distinctive feature of these principles, in Kalecki's version published by the Institute, was the reflux theory of profits, which showed how the retained profits of companies were dependent upon capitalists' own expenditure and the fiscal deficit of the government.[25] This was a crucial breakthrough for Breit, modifying, if not entirely replacing, his earlier Austrian notion of profits based on the presumed greater productivity of 'more roundabout' theories of production.

In 1935 Breit published a theory of the structure of interest rates in a paper that appeared in the German *Zeitschrift für Nationalökonomie*. The paper has a significance that goes far beyond the now relatively obscure debates in German monetary economics of the 1930s. The paper amounted to a substantial critique of the Cambridge (and Oxford) doctrine of Liquidity Preference that came to dominate monetary economics following the publication of Keynes' *General Theory*, a doctrine that is represented in Breit's paper by two of Hicks's early papers in monetary theory. Breit criticised the notion that this will give rise to an 'equilibrium' term structure of interest rates in credit markets. The grounds of his critique are that any actual structure of interest rates will also affect the financing preferences of non-financial corporations. The influence of the rate of interest on investment is therefore mediated through these balance sheet effects. But the aspect of the paper that has most currency in today's monetary and financial economics is Breit's examination of the effects of risk and uncertainty upon entrepreneurial investment and financing arrangements. Some of this corresponds to Keynes' distinction between lender's and borrower's risk, in Chapter 11 of his *General Theory*. However, Breit's exposition of how credit markets and financing contracts accommodate risk and uncertainty by raising interest rates and rationing credit is much closer to that of the New Keynesians.[26]

Important differences between more modern approaches and that of Breit should be emphasised. This relates in particular to the New Keynesians and to Tobin, whose 'q' theory is supposed to include corporate balance sheets in a portfolio theory of money and credit.[27] The modern approach limits the possible influence of the financial markets by adhering to the Miller–Modigliani doctrine that the *composition* of a company's financial liabilities (as opposed to their cost) cannot influence its investment activity. Tobin and the New Keynesians provide determinate solutions in general equilibrium models in which real rates of interest determine corporate investment and hence macroeconomic outcomes. By contrast, Breit used the *market* rates of interest actually available to an individual entrepreneur. He was therefore able to bring his analysis closer to industrial reality. Breit also highlighted the fact that the absence of a positive solution may lead to the extinction of the market for long-term securities. In this respect his is a *disequilibrium* model. It obviously arose out of the European reality of his time. Recent difficulties in reviving activity in Japan since the 1990s suggest that Breit's analysis may also be close conceptually, if not historically, to our reality as well, and may bring additional considerations to bear on dilemmas of contemporary monetary policy.[28]

The model in Breit's paper relates financial risk to the amount of borrowing that is undertaken by an individual firm. The larger is the amount the firm borrows, the greater is the charge on its own capital if the return on the invested loan falls below the interest charged. 'Financial risk' therefore increases with the size of the loan, relative to the entrepreneur's capital. Accordingly, above a certain size of loan, the lender takes into account this financial risk by charging a risk margin on top of the basic lending rate of interest. This margin increases with the excess of the loan. This article established the distinction between internal funds, the savings of the business, and external funds borrowed or raised from a financial intermediary. Those internal funds are drawn from the retained profits that in turn are derived largely by companies' own expenditure on investment (see Chapter 11 below).

This possibility that excessive external financing of business increases enterprises' risk is what distinguishes the analysis of risk in Breit, and subsequently also in Kalecki, Steindl and Minsky, from that of Hicks or Keynes. In an early paper on monetary theory, to which Breit referred, Hicks had argued that holders of financial assets assess the future value of their assets probabilistically, with uncertainty being reflected in the dispersion of possible future values.[29] In his *General Theory* Keynes had called this *lender's risk*, and distinguished it from *borrower's risk*, namely the possibility of an adverse outcome to the investment project for which finance is being raised, and for which the *borrower* is liable. Keynes merely hinted that the lender's risk may be reduced 'where the borrower is so strong and wealthy that he is in a position to offer an exceptional margin of security' and that, during a boom, 'the popular estimation of both these risks, both borrower's risk and lender's risk, is apt to become unusually and imprudently low'.[30]

Breit's paper is mostly concerned with how entrepreneurs decide between long-term and short-term loans in financing their 'new combinations'. On the one hand, long-term finance involves additional risk for the lender, in committing himself to a company that may get into financial difficulties, which would affect the resale value of long-term securities. The long-term lender therefore charges an additional premium for such finance. On the other hand, short-term finance involves what Breit called 'transformation' costs, or costs of rolling over short-term obligations (including the possibility of higher interest rates in the future). Given the external finance that is required, it is the balance between the short-term rate of interest plus these transformation costs, and the long-term rate with its risk premium that determines whether the entrepreneur will seek finance in the long-term or the short-term market.

In his paper, Breit concluded that business investment rather than conditions in credit markets held the key to improving business cash flow, and hence its prospects. This could be assisted by public works, which would have a similar effect on business liquidity. With this Breit rejected his Schumpeterian and Wicksellian origins, in which the rate of interest and the 'natural' productivity of (marginal) 'new combinations' were the key determining variables in the business up-swing.[31] But once the credit market lost its significance for investment, Breit was close to arguing a 'reflective' view of finance:

> It is not the difference between the high capital market interest rate, and the low money market interest rate, that is responsible for the reduction in investment activity. Instead, both the low volume of investment and the divergence of interest rates represent different symptoms of the same economic processes which operate at a much deeper level. It has also been shown that the divergence in interest rates is associated neither with intensity of the tendency towards liquidity in the economy, nor with the unequal division of demand [for credit] between the markets for long and short-term loans ... It

has been shown that the apparently low short-term interest rate is by no means low in an economic sense. Instead (together with transformation costs) it is excessive in comparison to the profitability of new enterprise. Above all, we have been able to refute the idea that the impulse which produces a new wave of prosperity must come directly from the credit market. In our reasoning, the fall in the rate of interest, and the increase in demand do not necessarily have to precede, either logically or in time, the growth in intensity of real economic processes. In certain cases, of course, both phenomena run in parallel. But in other ones, (for example, with the emergence of new combinations in production, or with counter-cyclical state investments), the fall in the rate of interest and the increasing liquidity of the markets are shown to be the consequence of increasing investment activity, whose rise is quite independent of the situation in the credit market.[32]

The publishing life of Marek Breit spanned no more than four years, and his writing life in economics no more than six. However, these were years when the economy that he was studying most directly swung between inflation and severe economic depression. In analysing both he identified banking and finance as crucial and relatively autonomous factors driving the inflationary and deflationary processes in the economy. Ultimately, he criticised credit cycle theories and the notions of liquidity preference in financial markets that were emerging in England, that were to culminate in Keynes's *General Theory*. Working with Kalecki, he came to a view that emphasised the liquidity of business balance sheets as the key to the fixed capital investment that drove the economic cycle.

NOTES

1.   Chilosi 1982.
2.   Kowalik 1992.
3.   Breit and Lange 1934.
4.   Kowalik 1992, p. 161.
5.   Breit 1933, pp. 3–5.
6.   Ibid., p. 214.
7.   Ibid., chapters IX and X.
8.   Ibid., p. 165.
9.   Ibid., p. 155.
10. Ibid., pp. 151–154.
11. Ibid., Chapter X; Hayek 1935.
12. Breit 1933, pp. 7–10.
13. Schumpeter 1934, chapters I and III.
14. See Ellis 1934, pp. 317–325.
15. Breit 1933, pp. 43–44.
16. Ibid., pp. 41–51.

17. Ibid., pp. 34–35.
18. White 1984.
19. Meulen 1934; Hayek 1976.
20. Realfonzo 1998, pp. 148–150.
21. Breit 1933, pp. 42, 46.
22. Goodhart 1987 and 1988, chapters 5 and 7.
23. Breit 1933, p. 197.
24. Breit 1935b.
25. Kalecki 1933b; see also Chapter 11 below.
26. E.g. Stiglitz and Weiss 1981.
27. Tobin 1969; Tobin and Brainard 1977. The inconsistencies in Tobin are explored in Chick 1983, pp. 213–217.
28. Some of these more recent problems are discussed in Goodhart 2001.
29. Hicks 1935.
30. Keynes 1936, pp. 14–15.
31. In a review of Breit's paper, at the conference of the European Society for the History of Economic Thought on 28 February 2004 in Treviso, Italy, Harald Hagemann pointed out that Breit's conclusion, in which he refers to 'new combinations' as *preceding* a fall in the rate of interest and a rise in the liquidity of the financial markets, is consistent with a Wicksellian view. This is correct, but Breit also mentions other factors, including public works, which could stimulate investment. Breit indicates that this investment itself is the cause of greater profits. Such profits too could be interpreted as a kind of Hayekian 'forced saving'.
32. '... nicht der Abstand zwischen dem hohen Stande des Kapitalmarkt- und dem niedrigen des Geldmarktzinsfußes daran die Schuld trägt, daß sich die Investierungstätigkeit verringert. Vielmehr stellen sowohl das kleine Investierungsvolumen, als auch die Zinsfußdivergenz verschiedene Symptome derselben viel tiefer verlaufenden wirtschaftlichen Vorgänge dar. Es zeigte sich weiter, daß die Zinsfußdivergenz weder mit der Intensität der Tendenz zur Liquidität der Wirtschaft, noch mit der ungleichmäßigen Verteilung der Nachfrage zwischen den lang- und kurzfristigen Märkten in Zusammenhang steht ... Es zeigte sich, daß der scheinbar niedrige kurzfris- tige Zinsfuß in wirtschaftlichen Sinne keineswegs gering ist, vielmehr is er (zusammen mit den Transformationkosten), im Vergleich mit der Rentabilität neuer Unternehmungen, übermäßig aufgetrieben. Am wichtig- stenist aber, daß wir im Stande waren, die Auffassung zu widerlegen, daß der Stoß, der eine neue Aufschwungswelle zeigt, unmittelbar von Seiten des Kreditmarktes erfolgen müsse. Das Sinken des Zinsfußes und das Steigen der Nachfrage müssen nach unseren Ausführungen weder im logischen, noch im zeitlichen Sinne dem Anwachsen der Intensität realer wirtschaftlicher Prozesse vorangehen. In gewissen Fällen laufen zwar die beiden Erscheinungen parallel ab, in anderen dagegen (z. B. bein Entstehung neuer produktiver Kombinationen oder bein konjunktureller Intervention durch staatliche Investierungen) erweisen sich das Sinken des Zinsfußes und die Verflüssigung der Marktes nur als Folgeerscheinungen der zune- hmenden Investierungstätigkeit, daren Ansteigen ganz unabhängig von

den Änderungen der Situation des Kreditmarktes angebahnt wurde' (Breit 1935a, pp. 658–659).

9. The principle of increasing risk: Michał Kalecki

Kalecki rapidly took up and extended the essential concept of financial risk that Breit had put forward. The first version of Kalecki's Principle of Increasing Risk appeared in English in 1937.[1] In his hands this analysis became a theory of investment, an explanation for the size of firms, and a reason why increasing the supply of credit in financial markets would not increase investment, as suggested by the equilibrium loanable funds theory.[2] Along the way he echoed (unconsciously) Fisher to criticise Pigou's real balance effect.

9.1   RISK IN CORPORATE FINANCE

Kalecki suggested that a constant prospective return on investment is more realistic than the decreasing returns favoured by marginalist economists. Given such a return, and the current rate of interest with increasing risk margins, the amount of investment that a firm can undertake is limited by the amount of its savings. A similar risk constraint would apply to funds raised from the stock market, through a rising cost of funds on bond issues. In the case of shares, existing shareholders would resist the watering-down of their stock by additional stock issues, and companies would be faced with rising costs of selling more than an 'optimum size of issue'.

In the 1954 version of this paper, Kalecki dropped the static analysis of investment decisions based on internal savings, and turned his Principle of Increasing Risk into a theory of the size of the firm under the revised title of 'Entrepreneurial Capital and Investment'.[3] He argued in general terms that 'the expansion of the firm depends on its accumulation of capital out of current profits',[4] and discussed the limitations of capital market finance. Bond issues reduce the return on share capital if the investment they finance is unsuccessful, while share issues reduce the control of the controlling shareholders. The latter may be partially overcome by a holding company structure (floating off up to 49 per cent of

a subsidiary). But the problem remains that, if the venture is unsuccessful, earnings per share will be reduced. Finally Kalecki suggested that
portfolio diversification by rentiers will limit the amount of new shares
in a company to which financial investors will be willing to subscribe.
He pointed out that all of these difficulties may be overcome through the
accumulation of internal savings from profits, i.e. entrepreneurial capital.
This provides a cushion of reserves to reduce the financial risk of capital
subscribers and will even 'widen the capital market for the shares of that
company since, in general, the larger a company is the more important
will its role in the share market be'.[5]

Readers versed in modern finance theory will immediately recognise
Kalecki's analysis of the limitations of external finance for investment
as an argument that the capital market is 'imperfect', i.e. it does not
automatically supply finance at the current price of finance, including
the risk premium of the *project* not the *firm*, for all projects with returns
in excess of that price. In the capital markets of the second half of
the twentieth century (or at least from the 1960s onwards), Kalecki's
constraints on capital finance have been barely detectable. However,
this is not because the capital markets have become more perfect, but
because of the inflation of those markets with pension fund savings. This
inflation has greatly enlarged the possibilities of capital market-financed
company growth. Where such growth has taken place, it has not been due
to increased productive investment, as the loanable funds theory would
predict. Rather it has been through waves of merger and takeover activity
that have increased industrial concentration and made capital markets
less stable.

Kalecki also intervened in the debate around Keynes's notion of an
under-employment equilibrium with an argument that Fisher would have
recognised. Arthur Pigou criticised this notion on the grounds that if
wages and prices were sufficiently flexible, then unemployment would
result in falling wages and prices. The resulting increase in the real value
of wealth, especially money holdings, in relation to current production,
would cause an increase in expenditure, which would bring the economy
back to a full employment equilibrium. This is known today as the 'Real
Balance Effect'. Kalecki pointed out that, unless those savings were held
in government debt or gold, the increase in the real value of savings due
to falling prices would mean an increase in the real value of private sector
debt. This would lead to corporate collapse, a crisis of confidence, and
industrial decline.[6]

Kalecki's real debt deflation view was evidently a relatively recent conclusion. Earlier, in a review of a book on monetary economics by the German economist E. Lukas, *Die Aufgaben des Geldes*, Kalecki had put forward a disequilibrium view of how the financial markets work, without mentioning the possibility that falling prices would entail a rise in the real value of corporate debt. The review also reveals how limited was the influence of Keynes in the work of the Polish economist whose correspondence with Joan Robinson is testimony to his resistance to Keynes's approach to macroeconomics.[7] Lukas's support for Nazi employment policies is noted without comment. Kalecki reserved his detailed criticisms for Lukas's exposition of the loanable funds theory that had been popularised in the English-speaking world by Dennis Robertson, and which formed the rationale for opposition to government expenditure on public works to alleviate mass unemployment. Robertson had equated bank credit with saving and argued that saving would normally evoke equivalent investment and held this view well after it had apparently been discredited by Keynes.[8] Kalecki wrote:

> The author (i.e., Lukas) takes for granted the popular view that the buying of securities by the saver automatically creates a demand for new capital equipment. Thus the increase in saving, as such, is not considered to have a 'deflationary' effect. If, however, savers buy, for example, bills, instead of bonds, a corresponding amount of purchasing power is shifted from the capital to the money markets and meets there a part of the demand for credits.[9] Thus credits granted by monetary authorities fall off and 'the purchasing power in circulation' shrinks *pro tanto*. As a result the fall in the demand for new capital equipment which occurs is not compensated for by the increase of effective demand in other parts of the economy. This description is, of course, inadequate. The process concerned is much more complicated. A shift of a certain amount (whether coming from new or old savings) from the capital to the money market tends to raise the long-term rate of interest, and thus reduce the volume of investment, but in general not just by the amount initially shifted.[10]

Kalecki here showed how, even with supply and demand equal in the bond and the money markets an increase in saving may transmit a deflationary impulse to the real economy through the normal and even efficient functioning of the financial system. At this time he still followed Keynes in regarding the long-term bond market as the market for finance of industrial investments, so that a shift of funds away from that market would cause a rise in long-term bond yields and an increase in the financing costs of new industrial investments, effectively discouraging such investments. The more interesting argument is, however, the way in which Kalecki may be said to have stood Hawtrey and Robertson on their heads, by showing how an increase in short-term saving can reduce the money supply. The buying of bills or, more generally, a rise in bank deposits, would merely result in a correspondingly lower demand from commercial banks accommodating credit from the central bank. An increase in saving thus induces a *reduction* in the money supply of the central bank. The money market rate of interest would not fall because a lower demand for central bank credits is met by a reduced supply of them *at the current rate*. The failure of the short-term rate to fall means that there is no incentive to switch savings back to the long-term bond market to obtain a new equilibrium there at the lower yield that would encourage higher investment.

Kalecki's model here suggests a structure of financial markets in which short-term interest rates are more stable than long-term rates, because central banks 'accommodate' changes in the demand for money in the money markets. In fact the reverse is the case: long-term rates tend to be more stable than short-term rates. This had been widely noted, by Harrod in *The Trade Cycle*, for example, and Hawtrey in *A Century of Bank Rate*. A large part of the debt of the British government had been consolidated at the end of the eighteenth century into irredeemable stocks, known as Consolidated Funds, or 'Consols' bearing a rate of interest of 2.5 per cent or 4 per cent of nominal value. The yield on Consols therefore varied with the price of the stock, but its period to maturity did not fall over time, as it would for a stock with a finite redemption date. That yield was therefore a variable price for a stock of constant immaturity, a pure yield unaffected by imminent repayment. With no default risk, because interest was payable by the British government indefinitely, the yield on Consols was commonly taken as the standard current return, on risk-free long-term stocks and the 'benchmark' for returns in long-term stocks.[11] Relatively stable yields on Consols over more than a hundred years were convincing evidence of the comparatively limited movement of long-term interest rates. The discussions of Consol yields by Harrod and Hawtrey feature among the very few references that Kalecki made in his work to other economists, and in his writing about the long-term rate of interest, he used the yield on Consols as the model for the long rate.

9.2   THE YIELD CURVE

Kalecki first wrote about this difference between the two ends of the yield curve in 1938, when preparing his *Essays in the Theory of*

Economic Fluctuations for publication. He added a brief chapter on 'The Long-Term Rate of Interest'. The purpose of the chapter was to show that the long-term rate is more stable than the short-term rate. He explained why this is the case by arguing that interest arbitrage between the two ends of the curve will not maintain a constant slope of the curve, but that the slope will vary as changes in the short-term rate of interest move the short end of the curve above or below a more constant long end of the curve:

> [In the course of an economic boom] an increase in investment causes the banks to sell bills and bonds in order to be able to expand advances ... The Central Bank, in buying bills reduces very much the pressure of sales ... But the effect of the Central Bank's buying is partly counterbalanced by the fact that with increasing activity the demand for notes 'in circulation' rises. At any rate there is an inherent tendency in the system for strong fluctuations in the discount rate, which in fact often makes itself felt.[12]

The reason why interest arbitrage will not equalise the two rates, with due allowance for factors such as risk, uncertainty, illiquidity, inflation etc., is because the current short-term rate of interest is not the short-term equivalent or opportunity cost of the long rate. That equivalent or opportunity cost is the average short-term rate expected over the term of the bond. Kalecki used as his representative financial investor 'a capitalist with a "non-speculative outlook"'. This may well be a reference to Keynes's recent distinction between 'speculation', i.e. investing for capital gains, and 'enterprise', investing for future income, in the stock market in Chapter 12 of his *General Theory*. If Kalecki too had such a distinction in mind then it would be entirely consistent with his methodological predilection for assuming rationality on the part of capitalists, rather than speculative fervour or existential indecision in the face of uncertainty. Kalecki wrote as follows:

> Consider a capitalist with a 'non-speculative outlook,' who faces the alternatives of holding his reserves in bonds or deposits. There is the advantage of a stable and generally higher income on the side of bonds: on the other hand, deposits are constant in value, while the price of bonds, in the case of emergency which may necessitate their sale in the indefinite future cannot be foreseen, and the risk of loss is always present. Thus it is clear that the stimulus to keep bonds is the margin between the *present* long-term rate and the anticipated *average* short-term rate over a long period. Now it is very likely that the change in the present rate on deposits does not greatly affect the expectations of its average over a long period. Thus it is plausible that

a deposit owner of the type considered may be induced to buy bonds though the rate on deposits has increased more than the yield on bonds.[13]

Kalecki may have developed this idea from his reading of Hawtrey's *A Century of Bank Rate* to which Kalecki referred as providing supporting evidence of the stability of the long-term bond rate. On page 147 of that book, Hawtrey cited evidence which the banker Samuel Gurney gave to a Parliamentary Committee in 1848. When asked what would be the effect of 'dear money', i.e. high short-term interest rates, on long-term interest rates, Gurney replied that this 'depends on how long dear money is expected to last'. If they were expected to last a long time, then long-term bond prices may fall, and the yields on those stocks rise in line with the rise in short-term interest rates. While it is unlikely that this account inspired Kalecki's explanation of the relative stability of long-term interest rates (Kalecki's interests were considerably more contemporary), Gurney's evidence in 1848 does corroborate Kalecki's view remarkably.

Kalecki drew two conclusions from the relative stability of long-term rates of interest. First of all, 'It excludes these theories of the business cycle which attribute the breakdown of prosperity to the increase of the rate of interest. For the rate of interest can stop the boom only by hampering investment, and it is chiefly the long-term rate which matters in investment activity.'[14] This was a sweeping dismissal of monetary theories of the business cycle, such as those of Hawtrey and Hayek. His second conclusion was:

> That the boom ends in general before full employment is reached. When the system comes to the point of full employment, wages must rise sharply. But ... this does not tend to reduce employment directly ... wages and prices continue to climb up, the demand for bank advances steadily increases, causing a strong rise in the short-term rate and – at least after a certain time – an appreciable increase in the long-term rate. Only this can overcome 'inflation' by hampering investment and stopping the rise in wages and prices.[15]

This analysis was incorporated by Kalecki in papers which were then combined for publication in his *Studies in Economic Dynamics* which then became his *Theory of Economic Dynamics: An Essay on Cyclical and Long-Run Changes in Capitalist Economy*, published respectively in 1943 and 1954, by which time Kalecki had dropped the reference to the 'non-speculative' capitalist. However, he had expanded his reasoning about the yield curve from his 'Lukas critique', with a static model in which the bond yield moves around the more stable short-term rate, due to the accommodating policy of central banks, to a more normal yield curve in which discretionary policy by monetary authorities moves short-term interest rates around the more stable bond rate. 'Call money', the automatic credit granted to brokers in the stock market would act as a further stabilising influence on bond yields, since such facilities would make brokers more ready to absorb excess supplies of bonds.

It is obvious that in a capitalist economy with markets for financial instruments kept stable by accommodating credit policies, the long-term bond yield and money market interest rates (hence also the yield curve in general) are inelastic with respect to the supply of saving. Keynes too was concerned to show how the long-term bond rate is inelastic. He attributed this to liquidity preference, i.e. the subjective unwillingness of savers to hold their money in financial assets without immediate assured liquidity. For Kalecki the reasons for the inelasticity of the yield curve in general were much more like the ones that Breit had put forward (see previous chapter). These were rooted in the institutional arrangements surrounding the operations of the money market. Inflows of savings or liquidity into the money market or the banking system, whether from additional saving or from the long-term bond market, merely reduce the credit supplied by the central bank. A switch of funds from the bond market to the money market would raise financing costs in the bond market, without reducing them in the money market. But by implication, a switch of funds from the money market or the banking system to the bond market has the capacity to reduce bond financing costs without increasing interest rates in the money market. Such a switch to the long-term securities market would be accommodated by the central bank.[16]

Kalecki put forward another reason why the financial markets would not automatically bring a finance capitalist economy into equilibrium. This is the inelasticity of rentiers' saving. In his *Studies in Economic Dynamics*, published in 1943, Kalecki suggested that, because of their high and stable incomes, rentiers always have positive saving, except when subjected to hyperinflation. In a closed economy, with no government, saving can be divided up between rentiers' saving, and the financial accumulation of companies (depreciation plus retained profits). *Ex post* saving, in Kalecki and Keynes, is equal to, and determined by, gross investment (see Chapter 6 above). When that investment falls, in a recession, so too does saving, and at the same rate as investment. If, however, rentiers' saving does not fall as fast, then the financial accumulation of companies must fall more rapidly than the fall in saving and investment overall. In effect, as a rising proportion of companies' investment is externally financed, their financial risk is increased. Firms may try to accommodate this by economising on their internal liquidity through reducing investment still further. In this way they reduce the financial accumulation of firms as a whole, and increase firms' external indebtedness still further.[17]

Because of this inelasticity, rentiers' saving tends to make recessions more extreme, introducing a 'negative trend' into Kalecki's business cycle model. However, when he revised his model, in the early 1950s, Kalecki pointed out that this negative trend is offset by technological innovations which stimulate investment. He argued that it is the net overall effect of rentiers' saving and innovations that determines the long-run development of capitalism.[18] This seems perhaps even more obvious at the end of the twentieth century than it did when Kalecki wrote his analysis.

When Kalecki was preparing *Essays in the Theory of Economic Fluctuations* for publication, in 1938, George Shackle was one of Kalecki's few friends in London and one of the small number of economists with whom he discussed his ideas. Although they did not correspond, so that there is no record of exchanges between them, Shackle kept a copy of the *Essays* and gave a glowing review in *Economica* to the *Studies in Economic Dynamics*. He also kept a copy of Kalecki's paper 'The Short-Term Rate and the Long-Term Rate' which appeared in the *Oxford Economic Papers* in 1940. Shackle was very methodical in his reading, annotating his books and papers carefully in pencil and even noting the date when he read a particular work. He first read Kalecki's paper on 28 October 1940, and he appears to have been particularly taken with Kalecki's idea that only some fraction of the current money market rate of interest enters into the expected rate of interest. He wrote at the bottom of the paper 'One of Kalecki's brilliant tours de force.'[19]

But when Shackle came to look at the yield curve he came to different conclusions that were much more in line with Kalecki's analysis in the Lukas review. Looking at the yields on different maturities of government bonds, against money market rates on particular days between 1945 and 1947, Shackle found that the longer bond rates varied more than the short rates. This he attributed to the anchoring down of short-term interest rates by the Bank of England's cheap money policy at this time, while what he called the 'violent movements' of the longer bond rates were caused, in his view, by fluctuations in the uncertainty of financial investors.[20]

9.3   THE SAVING CONFUSION

Kalecki's analysis of yield curve was a part of his realisation that the rate of interest could not be a factor in investment, and hence in the business cycle. These depended, in his view, on the rate of profit and the amount of 'entrepreneurial savings', i.e. the accumulated financial reserves of businesses. His closest associate in Britain, Joan Robinson, did not agree. Together with Keynes she had been wedded to the more orthodox Marshallian notion that, as the opportunity cost of fixed capital investment, the rate of interest had to be a factor in such investment. In 1952 she wrote 'My chief difference from Mr. Kalecki is in respect of his treatment of finance as the short-period bottleneck.'[21] In 1951, she had sent him a manuscript with a request for comments containing the caveat 'It disagrees with your system in not taking Finance as the limit.'[22]

It is impossible to tell from their correspondence what this manuscript was. But Robinson had recently published her essay on 'The Rate of Interest' and this paper gives some idea of her disagreement with Kalecki. In her essay she put forward a view of the yield curve in 'equilibrium' depending on the degree of uncertainty over capital values (affecting the bond yields) as opposed to uncertainty over short-term interest rates (affecting money market rates). The equilibrium between them is supposed to arise when investors will no longer engage in arbitrage between the two rates: 'Operations such as this to some extent smooth out differences in demand for securities of different types and bring the various interest rates closer together.'[23] An increase in the money supply 'given the state of expectations' would tend to push all rates down, but short rates more than longer rates (Robinson was of course writing before the Rational Expectations Revolution narrowed the scope of expectations to the money supply). An increase in investment raises money market rates and bond rates, because of the increased demand for money for transactions in the real economy. But prices of company shares (common stocks) would tend to rise in line with the increased optimism associated with higher investment. An increase in saving ('thriftiness') has an immediate impact on stocks and causes retailers to require additional money from the banking system and through the sale of bonds in a way that Hawtrey probably recognised at the time the paper was published. But after excess retail stocks have been sold, and with a constant supply of money, interest rates would eventually fall, most of all in the money market, and the dispersion of yields on company shares would increase as share prices fall due to falling sales. But she concluded that: 'This pattern of interest rates does not look very encouraging to investment … investment must be revised in the downward direction because of the surplus capacity and low profits in the consumption trades and the high cost of industrial borrowing.'[24]

Joan Robinson's insistence on the rate of interest as a factor in investment decisions, and her assumption that the monetary authorities would hold the money supply constant, were bringing her very close to the 'loanable funds' position (in which the rate of interest naturally equilibrates saving and investment) which she may have identified in Kalecki's Principle of Increasing Risk. Her objections to Kalecki's 'finance bottleneck' centred around her worry that this was equivalent to the 'loanable funds' view that savings generate their own investment and hence that Say's Law holds. She was not the only economist to make this inference. None other than Dennis Robertson, the rival of the Keynes circle at Cambridge and evangelist of the 'loanable funds' gospel quoted from Kalecki's 1949 *Review of Economic Studies* paper 'A New Approach to the Problem of Business Cycles' the following sentence:

> A reasonable interpretation of the inter-relation between the level of income and investment decisions should be based, I think, on the fact that with a high level of income there is correlated a high level of savings, and that the stream of new savings stimulates investment because it makes it possible to increase investment without increasing indebtedness.

Robertson was delighted to find coming from the pen of someone regarded as a heavyweight Keynesian words that could be used to confirm his equilibrium analysis and his criticism of Keynes. 'Induced savings of the public' will find 'a vent in real investment either directly or through the machinery of a normally functioning stock exchange'.[25] '… Highbrow opinion', he now remarked:

> is like a hunted hare; if you stand in the same place, or nearly the same place, it can be relied upon to come round to you in a circle. What then was my joy to find, a couple of years ago, that Mr. Kalecki, than whose no brow is higher, had been struck by this same thought that the induced saving might walk away and generate investment on its own … It is not so much investment which governs savings as savings which govern investment.[26]

In his response to Joan Robinson, Kalecki insisted that what he had in mind was not savings in general, but the savings of the entrepreneur.

Rising indebtedness would tend to reduce investment, as would the fall in the rate of profit attendant upon higher saving:

> If, with a given distribution of savings (between rentiers and entrepreneurs) the level of savings is reduced, then [an] entrepreneur will be *ceteris paribus* reducing the volume of his investment decisions, because if he continued to invest at the same level, he would tend to increase his indebtedness ... Investment decisions are a function not only of current entrepreneurial savings, but also of the change in the factors determining the rate of profit ... If the rate of profit is increasing, investment will be higher than when it is constant, and the entrepreneur will be able to secure the finance for that in such a case. It is assumed that at the end of each period the entrepreneur has undertaken all such investment plans which he considered profitable and for which he could obtain finance. What makes him undertake investment in the next period is the new supply of his own savings, and the change in the rate of profit.[27]

Joan Robinson did not raise again the question of finance with Kalecki, and dropped references to her differences with him over this in her writings about him. Her subsequent references to Kalecki were characterised by even more warmth and respect. But she did not take into her work his disequilibrium analysis of finance. Its development was left to Kalecki's colleague, Josef Steindl.

NOTES

1. Kalecki 1937.
2. See Chilosi 1982; Mott 1982, 1985–1986.
3. Kalecki 1954, Chapter 8.
4. Ibid., p. 92.
5. Ibid., p. 94.
6. Kalecki 1944; see also Sawyer 1985, Chapter 5, and Sawyer 2001.
7. Joan Robinson wrote to Kalecki in September 1936 '... you are making an attack on Keynes ... Keynes's system you say is unrealistic ...' (Osiatyński 1990, p. 502). In his review of Keynes's *General Theory* in that same volume of the *Collected Works of Michał Kalecki* (Osiatyński 1990) Kalecki gave a full explanation of why in his view Keynes was only partially right.
8. Robertson 1928 and 1949.
9. Kalecki refers here to pages 408–410 of Lukas's book. Kalecki means here that, buying bills instead of bonds, demand for securities shifts to the money market, where banks may sell bills to savers. 'Savers' do not, of course, operate directly in the money markets, but through intermediaries, e.g. insurance companies or pension funds.
10. Kalecki 1938, p. 77.

11. In fact Consols were not so strictly irredeemable: at various times, the British government contributed to Sinking Funds, dedicated to the repayment of its debt, and this affected the price and hence the yield of these stocks.
12. Kalecki 1939, pp. 111–112.
13. Ibid., pp. 112–113.
14. Ibid., pp. 114–115.
15. Ibid., p. 115.
16. See Hawtrey's theory of stock market bubbles, discussed in Chapter 4 above, and the theory of capital market inflation put forward in Toporowski 1993a, pp. 114–119. See also Toporowski 1999a, and Toporowski 2000, Chapter 2.
17. Kalecki 1943, pp. 85–86.
18. Ibid., p. 159.
19. I am grateful to Mrs Catherine Shackle for giving me George Shackle's copy of Kalecki's *Essays* and a copy of the page of Kalecki's paper with her husband's annotations.
20. Shackle 1949.
21. Robinson 1952, p. 159.
22. Osiatyński 1991, p. 538.
23. Robinson 1952, p. 11.
24. Ibid., p. 28. This last remark is inconsistent with the fall in the yield curve that Robinson had just described.
25. Robertson 1936.
26. Ibid.
27. Osiatyński 1991, p. 539.

10. The principle of increasing risk: Josef Steindl and Michał Kalecki on profits and finance

Josef Steindl worked with Kalecki in Oxford during the Second World War and was to regard him as the seminal influence on his work. Indeed, so great was Kalecki's influence that, in comparing their work, it is difficult to identify where that influence gave way to Steindl's own ideas. In his early papers, 'On Risk' and 'Capitalist Enterprise and Risk' Steindl put forward the Breit–Kalecki Principle of Increasing Risk, and suggested that it leads to 'capital-wastage' in small enterprises. However, in the second of the two papers he touched upon an issue which was to become a distinctive theme in his later work. He suggested that in the joint stock system, 'over-capitalization' or the issue of stock in excess of 'the cost value of real assets' is used to give 'inside' shareholders controlling the company a higher rate of profit and a greater influence over the company vis-à-vis 'outside' shareholders. Steindl's first book, *Small and Big Business: Economic Problems of the Size of Firms*, brought together the results of his work, at the Oxford Institute of Statistics and Nuffield College Oxford from 1943 to 1946, on the Courtauld Inquiry into business organisation. Like Steindl's other books, it is a critique of the Marshallian theory of the 'representative firm', and Steindl returned to the Principle of Increasing Risk as a factor limiting the effectiveness of lifting the financing constraint on small businesses. He also noted that 'over-capitalization' leads to the understatement of the rate of profit on the actual capital of big companies.[1]

10.1 MONOPOLY CAPITALISM AND INFLEXIBLE SAVING

Steindl's second book was his classic study of American monopoly capitalism in the six decades before the Second World War, *Maturity and Stagnation in American Capitalism*. With the Wall Street Crash playing something of a pivotal role in that period, consideration of the role of finance in economic stagnation was inevitable even though that consideration was overshadowed by the analysis of monopoly capitalism for which that book is best known. Having examined the boom that preceded the Crash, Steindl came to the conclusion that the equity market of the joint stock system can effectively enhance the entrepreneurial capital of big companies. With share prices determined by expected earnings per share, an inflow of funds into the market will tend to elicit new shares from companies, taking advantage of the cheaper finance.[2] This would offset the investment-reducing effect of the falling rate of profit as real capital expands.[3] Larger companies can issue shares more cheaply at lower yields. Therefore a capital market boom tends to encourage the emergence of monopolies through 'financial concentration'. In mergers and takeovers the lower-yielding shares of the larger company are issued in exchange for the higher-yielding shares of the company that is being bought out. Furthermore, the inflow of funds into the equity market allows the further development of holding company structures in which new shares may be issued without diluting the control of the dominant shareholders. In this way the 1920s stock market boom reinforced a tendency towards monopoly in American capitalism and offset a declining overall rate of profit during that decade. However, after the Crash, the market for new shares evaporated.

According to Steindl, the key mechanism by which financial inflation contributed to economic decline was through the monopolies that were created by webs of holding companies. Because they could exact a higher profit margin from their customers, monopolies were more willing to tolerate excess productive capacity. But having unused capacity also discouraged firms from investment in that capacity. Lower investment, in turn, led to economic stagnation.

In his 1982 paper on 'Household Saving in a Modern Economy', Steindl returned to the fundamental starting point of his analysis, and of the approach to finance of Kalecki and Breit, the Principle of Increasing Risk. The paper put forward the Principle as a macroeconomic issue affecting the balances of the various sectors (private households, the corporate sector, the public sector, and the overseas sector) in the flow of funds accounts. He started with the Keynesian saving identity. According to this, Saving is by definition equal to Gross Investment, plus the Government's Fiscal Deficit, plus the Trade Surplus. (This is further discussed below.) Steindl then distinguished between household saving and corporate saving. An increase in household saving, with the other factors remaining constant, leads to an 'enforced indebtedness of companies':

> Business will find that their profits have fallen below expectations, and they therefore have to finance their current investment to a greater extent than fore-seen by borrowing. This may then motivate them to reduce their investment in the future.[4]

The rising indebtedness of business would normally be offset by a rising trade surplus, and a rising fiscal deficit, because they are net inflows of funds into the business sector. But, in one respect, the analysis overall represents a significant divergence from Kalecki's own analysis. Steindl made clear that household saving has an immediate impact on corporate retained profits and saving, whereas in Kalecki's model household saving affects rather the 'trend' of economic activity.[5]

Finally, in an undated paper that appeared in the volume of his Collected Papers that was published in 1990, Steindl returned to the much more Keynesian theme of conventional valuations in the stock market. In his *Treatise on Money* discussion of how stock market activity affects bank deposits, Keynes had argued that when traders are buying and selling for capital gains (i.e. speculating) stock prices depend on balance between 'bullish' expectations that stock prices will rise, and 'bearish' expectations that prices will fall. Steindl put forward a model in which such views are brought to balance by price adjustments. If there is an excess of 'bullish' sentiment, buyers will raise prices until they change the expectations of sufficient 'bulls' to persuade them to become 'bears', or sellers of stock because they no longer expect further price increases. A 'total frequency distribution will show just how much funds are associated with each expected price'. He then introduced uncertainty in the form of the variance of price expectations that then affects the price elasticity of demand and supply in the market. If expectations are closely concentrated, a small price change will move a large volume of money between bulls and bears. If expectations are widely dispersed, a large change in price is necessary to get stocks and money circulating in the market. However, this analysis only holds if the price expectations of individuals are independent of each other. In practice there are 'opinion leaders' around whom expectations will 'cluster'. Such clusters are unstable as new 'opinion leaders' emerge. This leads to a second type of uncertainty, over 'the variety of possible clusters of opinion and the frequency of shifts between them'. Imitation may cause 'agglomerations in one or another direction' so that the market becomes 'bearish' or 'bullish'. Steindl suggests the possibility of a 'two-humped frequency distribution' with market opinion switching between two extremes, before concluding:

> The most extreme loss of independence occurs in a crash. Here one opinion has come to dominate and the other condition for steady state, the existence of a belief in certain limits or standards, has also disappeared.[6]

10.2   PROFITS AND FINANCE

In their writings, Michał Kalecki and Josef Steindl put forward two theoretical innovations that, combined, form a theory of financial cycles with certain acknowledged similarities to the theory that Hyman P. Minsky fashioned out of the work of John Maynard Keynes, but that is arguably more complete than Minsky's theory. These innovations were the Principle of Increasing Risk, which has been discussed here and in the previous two chapters, and the theory of profits, to which some consideration must now be given, since it remains a crucial influence on the course of business cycles in economies dominated by finance capital.

Kalecki's theory of profits is perhaps the oldest element of his economic analysis. It certainly pre-dates the Principle of Increasing Risk, which he had developed only after Breit's paper of 1935. The theory was pithily summarised by Kalecki's Cambridge partisan, Joan Robinson, although not by Kalecki himself, as 'the workers spend what they get; the capitalists get what they spend'.[7] She added, by way of explanation, that 'an increase in investment increases profits to whatever extent is required to raise saving out of profits to the corresponding extent', by which she meant that investment determines profits. The idea originally came to Kalecki as a result of his work on the national income accounts in Poland in 1930. But its origins go back to the economic reproduction schemes in volume II of Marx's *Capital*. It can also be detected as the substance behind Austrian theories of 'forced saving' and Wicksell's macroeconomics, which had become influential among Polish economists in the inter-war period.

The theory starts from the national income identity between total income and total expenditure in the economy in a given period (e.g. one year). If consumption is deducted from the income and expenditure sides of the equation, then the remainder is the sum of taxes, and saving. This is then equal to the sum of government expenditure, gross investment and the balance of trade surplus (exports minus imports). Transferring taxes over to the expenditure side gives the well-known 'Keynesian' saving identity, that is, saving equals Gross Investment (i.e. expenditure on plant machinery and stocks, rather than financial investment), plus the Fiscal Deficit (i.e. government expenditure minus taxes) plus the Trade Surplus.

All that may be concluded from this is that the amount of saving in an economy will always finance whatever investment, or deficit spending by the government, has taken place. By a small manipulation of this equation, Kalecki showed how profits are determined. For the sake of simplicity Kalecki introduced an assumption that there are only two classes in society: capitalists, who receive profits, and workers who earn wages. The saving identity therefore represents the saving out of profits *and* wages. If saving from wages is deducted from the expenditure side of the equation, then the identity represents just the saving out of profits. Since profits can only be spent on investment, or they can be consumed, or they can be saved, adding in consumption out of profits to the expenditure side, gives an equation for profits. Profits therefore, are equal to the sum of Gross Investment, plus the Fiscal Deficit, plus the Trade Surplus, plus Capitalists' Consumption minus Workers' Saving. Kalecki pointed out that this equation for profits is, of course, an identity derived from the national income identity between income and expenditure. By itself it has no causal implication. But it is, in fact, the expenditure side which determines the income (profit) side, because capitalists 'may decide to consume and to invest more in a given period than in the preceding one, but they cannot decide to earn more'.[8]

As a matter of empirical observation, of these elements, investment is the most important. The fiscal deficit, the trade surplus, and the balance between capitalists' consumption and workers' saving are balance items which would rarely exceed, say, 5 per cent of Gross Domestic Product. By contrast, gross domestic fixed capital formation, or investment expenditure, usually falls in the range of 15 per cent to 33 per cent of Gross Domestic Product.[9] This has two important implications for economic activity. First of all, profits are determined largely by other capitalists' or firms' expenditure, rather than the mark-ups that a firm impose on its cost of production. Even more importantly, this analysis shows that investment expenditure *automatically* generates the saving necessary to finance it:

> If some capitalists increase their investment by using for this purpose their liquid reserves, the profits of other capitalists will rise *pro tanto* and thus

the liquid reserves will pass into the possession of the latter. If the additional investment is financed by bank credit, the spending of the amounts in question will cause equal amounts of saved profits to accumulate as bank deposits. The investing capitalists will thus find it possible to float bonds to the same extent and thus to repay the bank credits.[10]

An important consequence of this is that the common view among economists that the investment of firms in the economy is somehow constrained by the amount of savings in the economy is at best only partially true. It applied to the early capitalists of whom Adam Smith and David Ricardo wrote, before the emergence of a 'national' economy in which capitalist enterprises are wholly integrated through markets, and, in particular, through the use of a common financial system. The saving constraint applies still to small and medium-sized businesses that have not been able to accumulate financial reserves, and in developing countries. But for the big businesses that account for the bulk of investment in an established capitalist economy, there is no saving constraint. There is instead the problem of financial risk. Kalecki concluded that:

> One important consequence of the ... [reflux theory of profits] is that the rate of interest cannot be determined by the demand for and the supply of new capital because investment 'finances itself'.[11]

Kalecki thereby placed himself with Keynes as a pioneer of a 'pure monetary' theory of interest, in which interest is no longer influenced, as in classical political economy, by the rate of profit on new investment. Moreover, Kalecki's conclusion that investment 'finances itself' in a financially integrated capitalist economy removes the main argument that has been repeatedly adduced since the emergence of financial markets for inflating those markets, namely that such inflation is 'necessary' to increase business investment.[12]

Kalecki's reflux theory of profits has been associated with Keynes's 'widow's cruse' analogy in the *Treatise on Money*. This association is worth examining, because it highlights an important difference between the two theorists concerning their respective views on the role of finance in the capitalist economy. The association has been made, for example, by Michael Howard in his book *Profits in Economic Theory*.[13] In his *Treatise*, Keynes wrote:

> There is one peculiarity of profits (or losses) which we may note in passing, because it is one of the reasons why it is necessary to segregate them from

income, as a category apart. If entrepreneurs choose to spend a portion of their profits on consumption (and there is, of course, nothing to prevent them from doing this), the effect is to *increase* the profit on the sale of liquid consumption goods by an amount exactly equal to the amount of profits which have been thus expended. This follows from our definitions, because such expenditure constitutes a diminution of saving ...Thus, however much of their profits entrepreneurs spend on consumption, the increment of wealth belonging to entrepreneurs remains the same as before. Thus profits, as a source of capital increment for entrepreneurs, are a widow's cruse which remains undepleted however much of them may be devoted to riotous living. When, on the other hand, entrepreneurs are making losses, and seek to recoup those losses by curtailing their normal expenditure on consumption, i.e., by saving more, the cruse becomes a Danaid jar which can never be filled up; for the effect of this reduced expenditure is to inflict on the producers of consumption goods a loss of an equal amount. Thus the diminution of their wealth, as a class, is as great, in spite of their savings, as it was before.[14]

The similarity with Kalecki's theory of profits arises from the common notion that 'capitalists receive what they spend'. However, in contrast to Kalecki, but like Marx in volume II of *Capital*, the reflux is of the money that capitalists spend on *consumption*, rather than investment.[15] Moreover, Keynes's reflux theory was in the context of an attempt to relate prices to the quantity of money in circulation. The implicit assumption underlying this was that the level of output remains constant, so that the change in capitalists' expenditure affects only prices. Keynes elicited criticism for this from Dennis Robertson, Friedrich Hayek and Austin Robinson, who termed it 'the widow's cruse fallacy'. Robinson questioned 'If an entrepreneur, loaded with profits, decided on his way home to have a shoe-shine, was the effect solely to raise the price of shoe-shines?'[16] Keynes's editor, Donald Moggridge, wrote that 'As a "general theory", rather than a statement of a particular limiting case, it was inadequate.'[17] The idea was, in any case, incidental to Keynes's quasi-Wicksellian analysis in the *Treatise*. The course of his discussions with Joan Robinson, Austin Robinson and Richard Kahn, in the Cambridge 'Circus' that was trying to bring systematic order into the medley of his ideas, directed Keynes elsewhere. This was towards the notion that changes in investment affect the economy through their influence on consumption in what became the orthodox Keynesian multiplier analysis.[18]

But, having dropped the reflux theory of profits, Keynes also lost with it the idea pressed by Kalecki, that capitalists' expenditure on investment and their own consumption reappears as profits, and hence that investment expenditure is, in general, not credit-constrained. The exceptions here are the early capitalist enterprises and small businesses that do not have the reserves to embark on investment, or Schumpeter's 'new combinations'.[19] These are, in any case, marginal to the investment undertaken in mature capitalist economies by large corporations with liquid assets. In response to a very similar argument to Kalecki's from Bertil Ohlin[20] Keynes introduced a new 'finance' motive for demanding money because:

> Planned investment – i.e. investment *ex ante* – may have to secure its 'financial provision' *before* the investment takes place; that is to say, before the corresponding saving has taken place.[21]

In later years this was to inspire among some post-Keynesians precisely what Kalecki sought to dismiss, namely the notion that somehow the market rate of interest, rather than income and expenditure, brings saving and investment into balance.[22]

10.3 THE LIQUIDITY PREFERENCE THEORY OF INVESTMENT

As has already been mentioned, Kalecki's theory of profits is in effect a reflux theory of investment, since it is investment that provides the bulk of the expenditure which enables profits to be realised. If investment determines the major share of profits, what determines investment? Kalecki worked on this question from the time when he published his first papers in economics until the end of his life. His published analysis changed in successive versions of his theory. But, there was a common core to all of them, around the Principle of Increasing Risk as a 'liquidity preference' theory of investment. Steindl showed this in his paper 'Some Comments on the Three Versions of Kalecki's Theory of the Trade Cycle' which, despite its title, is really about Kalecki's investment theories. As is well known, Keynes had put forward in his *General Theory* a liquidity preference theory of interest, according to which the liquidity preference of financial investors, or rentiers, determines the rate of interest that they will demand in order to part with immediate purchasing power when they lend money. Kalecki's Principle of Increasing Risk, as developed by Steindl, suggests a liquidity preference theory of *investment*.

According to this view companies are constrained in their investment in fixed capital by the need to keep sufficient liquid reserves and assets to be able to meet future cash commitments. But firms have two ways of regulating their internal liquidity, the basis of their ability to settle financial commitments. The first of these is by borrowing or raising new capital. This expands their future financial liabilities. The second way is by varying their investment commitments. Given the extended gestation period of fixed capital investment, varying investment commitments can only be done by postponing, or bringing forward, new investments. If a firm reduces its investment it is left with a greater amount of liquid reserves, for a given amount of outstanding financial liabilities. This increase in reserves will, of course, only be temporary if other firms pursue a similar course: as the investment reflux theory of profits shows, the effect of lower investment will be to reduce profits for firms as a whole. Nevertheless, because the costs of investment are charged, in the first instance, to the internal liquidity of the company, i.e. its liquid reserves and liquid assets, the individual firm's investment programme is managed in such a way as to maintain the internal liquidity of the firm. A rise in financial liabilities requires the firm to maintain a larger stock of liquid assets in order to meet future payments on those liabilities.

As for financing commitments, i.e. the issue of capital liabilities by companies in a financially developed capitalist economy, this is determined not so much by the financing requirements of fixed capital investments, as suggested by the finance theories of virtually all econ-omists, most notably Tobin, but also Keynes and possibly even Minsky (see Chapters 12 and 14 below). Rather it is determined by demand for financial assets, which companies as a whole can be induced to issue by the simple expedient of rising prices for financial assets. If firms do not have sufficient investment projects to absorb the finance that financial investors offer them, then rising securities prices (and the implied lower cost of finance) will eventually induce companies to issue new securities. The proceeds of these issues will then be used to reduce bank debt or to buy other securities, or simply kept as bank deposits. (The issue of long-term securities in order to pay off bank debt, a procedure known as 'funding', does not, of course, expand a firm's balance sheet. But it does stabilise the balance sheet by reducing the need to repay debt in the short term.[23] Of course, if the proceeds of new securities issued are used to buy other securities (in merger and acquisition activity, or management buy-outs) then this simply prolongs the boom in financial asset prices. Steindl recognised that a reduction in investment, relative to its financing, would result in additional 'enforced indebtedness' of companies, which would then reduce investment. He did not, however, explore the possibility implied by his analysis that a rise in financing, relative to investment, would eventually have the same effect.

A rise in saving represents a corresponding reduction in expenditure and income for firms and hence, as Steindl noted, an increase in the indebtedness (or a reduction in the internal liquidity) of companies. However, a rise in 'rentiers' savings' also represents an increase in the financial liabilities of companies, which issue additional capital or debt to absorb those increased savings. The increased financial liabilities will tend to depress investment.[24]

Companies with access to the capital market, i.e. those companies in the advanced capitalist countries that account for the vast majority of private sector investment, therefore face a dilemma when they undertake investment of uncertain profitability whose financing can drain their internal liquidity. They finance investment from internal liquidity, and then 'fund' this expenditure through the issue of new financial liabilities (stocks or bonds), to replenish internal liquidity, against completed investments of proven profitability. This is the basis of what I have else-where called the 'refinancing theory of capital markets'.[25] Refinancing is required because firms are not 'representative': they have different financial characteristics and operate in different markets. (Steindl under-took a pioneering statistical investigation of this in his book *Random Processes and the Growth of Firms*.) A given investment expenditure raises the profits of all firms in general. But the additional profits are distributed among firms according to their relative size and their degree of monopoly, which allows them to raise prices in response to a given increase in expenditure. Big businesses, that undertake the bulk of private sector investment, also have the greatest market power and, therefore, get the bulk of additional profits spread among themselves.[26]

Hence, a firm making an investment does not get back through the reflux (or Kahn/Keynes multiplier) process all that it spends on invest-ment. Firms in general will need to refinance investments, in order to replace the internal reserves spent on those investments. The refinancing of investments through the capital market makes companies vulnerable to the inflation of that capital market. The money that a company obtains from the issue of capital market securities is not 'free' liquidity, available for further investment. Some of it has to be held back against the possi-bility that in future existing productive capital may not generate the cash flow required to service the company's financial liabilities. This financial uncertainty can be accommodated by issuing stock in excess of what is required to refinance existing completed investments. Moreover, if stock prices are rising, as they would normally in a boom, a remunerative alternative to fixed capital investment emerges. The company's excess capital, and a large part of its liquid assets, can be used to buy stock issued by other companies, for later sale at a profit. Rising stock prices are usually the result of financial investment or placements that are in excess of the additional capital requirements of governments and companies. Using a company's excess capital for corporate acquisitions is a way of taking the excess liquidity that is causing the stock market boom out of the market and then putting it back into the market as additional purchases of securities. This then prolongs the boom in the stock market.

Moreover, it makes apparent sense to hold financial assets against growing financial liabilities: In a period of financial inflation they are more liquid than fixed capital investment, and their profits can be more quickly realised. There is a 'wealth effect' on consumption, as the higher incomes of financial intermediaries and personal investors finance luxury consumption. This personal prosperity accompanies a shift in the priorities of companies, from production and investment, towards corporate balance sheet restructuring as a way of generating speculative profits. This was a feature of recent economic booms in the United Kingdom and the United States. These booms were also marked by slow investment in traditional technologies alongside speculative investment in new technology. Such unbalanced growth was analysed perceptively by Kalecki in his last model of the business cycle.[27] In this way an investment boom, and the consequent rise in profits, give way to even more rapidly rising financial liabilities and a fall in net (retained) profits. These eventually deter investment, causing gross profits to fall as well. Thus the Principle of Increasing Risk implies two elements of financial disturbance in an economy, namely rising financial liabilities, and falling investment, relative to external financing, and hence profits.[28]

Steindl first put forward this idea in his *Maturity and Stagnation in American Capitalism*. He argued in Section 2 of Chapter IX that, overall, the saving in an economy is relatively inelastic. The balance between this *external indebtedness* of business, and the gross profits which finance the servicing of that indebtedness, has to be made up by additions to, or deductions from, the internal liquidity of companies. Companies, in turn, regulate their internal liquidity through the issue of long-term securities or by postponing investment projects. A reduction of investment, in accordance with Kalecki's reflux theory of profits, reduces profits. Steindl commenced his argument by arguing that rentiers' savings are especially inelastic.[29] He referred at this point to Kalecki's argument that 'the existence of rentiers' savings causes a negative long-run investment, i.e., long-run shrinking of capital equipment ... because this causes a continuous increase in entrepreneurs' indebtedness towards rentiers, which depresses investment activity'.[30] Steindl went on to argue that, to prevent rising indebtedness, reductions in saving therefore have to come from reducing the saving of the professional middle classes. This is unlikely since 'the savers in these groups are in relatively sheltered positions, and their income is not subject to very great pressure'.[31] As a consequence, the pressure of the adjustment of saving to investment has to come about through a reduction in economic activity, and hence a fall in employment.

> Whatever elasticity of outside savings there *might* be ... is dependent on unemployment. If therefore the real capital accumulation decreases, and it becomes necessary to reduce the rate at which outside savings accumulate in order to prevent a growing disequilibrium [i.e. rising indebtedness – JT], then a considerable increase in the degree of secular unemployment is practically the only means to this end ...
> If an increase in the degree of secular unemployment cannot bring about a sufficient reduction in the rate of outside saving ... then, instead of leading to a new 'moving equilibrium' the sequence of events conforms to the disequilibrium described above. Internal accumulation is reduced proportionately more than outside saving, so that the gearing ratio [between external financial liabilities and assets – JT] increases. Further reduction of investment will fall more heavily on internal accumulation than on outside savings, so that the gearing ratio increases. Real accumulation, internal accumulation, and the profit rate will thus continue to fall and the gearing ratio will continue to rise. The outstanding feature of this *disequilibrium* is that the gearing ratio *in fact* established is continuously out of harmony with the ratio entrepreneurs *wish* to establish: this indeed is the reason for the continuing disequilibrium. There is a growing relative indebtedness against the wish of entrepreneurs, one might say an 'enforced indebtedness'.[32]

The counterpart of the inelasticity of saving of the rentiers and the middle classes is a more extreme volatility of the financial accumulation of companies (depreciation plus retained profits).

Keynes had previously argued that changes in national income make saving adjust to investment *automatically*.[33] Steindl showed how this process takes time, and makes the economy move cumulatively through successive phases of disequilibrium, in which retained profits balance the inflexible response of household savers and rentiers to changes in investment. In effect it is a 'Wicksellian process' of falling investment and profits that continues as long as household and rentiers' saving leaves companies with inadequate retained profits to finance a stable level of investment. Steindl's notion of rising indebtedness may also be contrasted with Hayek's doctrine of 'forced saving'.[34] However, Hayek's forced saving is the excess of investment over voluntary saving, which then results in unplanned saving with no counterpart in unplanned debt. In Kalecki and Steindl, the reflux of investment comes to profits, and external indebtedness increases by the amount by which investment fell short of saving.

Steindl believed, like most economists, that the 1920s boom in the US stock market financed an investment boom, and that the fall off in the growth of that investment was due to the rise of monopolies, created by the corporate restructuring that accompanied the boom. A reconstruction of Kalecki's ideas was put forward in some of its essentials by Hyman P. Minsky (see Chapter 14), and in my book *The End of Finance*. But its elements were developed by Kalecki and Steindl well before the rise of finance in the second half of the twentieth century. A key role in their work was the idea that the saving of rentiers, far from providing additional financial resources for companies as orthodox finance theory suggests, actually destabilises the financial accumulation and internal liquidity of companies. At the end of the twentieth century the rentiers were financial institutions: pension and insurance funds that, with the proliferation of funded pension schemes through the 1990s and the 1990s, directed their large financial surpluses into markets for corporate financial liabilities. A system in which rentiers' saving has been not so much inelastic as upwardly elastic, with eventually devastating consequences for the cumulative financial liabilities of those funds as their surpluses were reduced. Although it is sound on the dynamics of financial deflation, Kalecki and Steindl's work provides limited directions for the understanding of financial inflation. The two major financial inflations of the twentieth century, the 1920s stock market boom in the United States and the financial boom of the final decades of the twentieth century, largely preceded or came after the period, from the 1930s to the 1960s, in which Kalecki and Steindl developed their main ideas. Nevertheless, the essential concepts for understanding the economic fragility induced by financial inflation, namely the fall in investment attendant upon enforced indebtedness and rising external liabilities, may be found in their work.

Steindl's most important work, *Maturity and Stagnation in American Capitalism*, was published in 1952. It brought to an end the analytical exposition of critical finance in the first half of the twentieth century. As a monograph concerned with a particular historic period through which American capitalism had passed, its discussion of economic stagnation also looked forward to the economic condition of the first decades of the twenty-first century.

NOTES

1. Steindl 1945b, p. 42.
2. Steindl 1952, p. 142.
3. Ibid., pp. 144, 153–154.
4. Steindl 1982.
5. Kalecki 1954, p. 159.
6. Steindl 1990.
7. Robinson 1969, p. ix.
8. Kalecki 1954, p. 46.
9. See Toporowski 1993b and 1999b.
10. Kalecki 1954, p. 50.
11. Ibid.
12. Victoria Chick has shown how changes in financing structures allow investment to determine saving in 'The Evolution of the Banking System and the Theory of Saving, Investment and Interest' (Chick 1986).
13. Howard 1983, pp. 161–163; see also Wood 1975.
14. Keynes 1930, vol. I, p. 139. See also Chapter 7 above.
15. Marx wrote: '… paradoxical as it may appear at first sight, it is the capitalist class itself which throws the money into circulation which serves for the realisation of the surplus value incorporated in the commodities. But, *nota bene*, it does not throw it into circulation as advanced money, hence not as capital. It spends it as means of purchase for its individual consumption' (Marx 1974, pp. 338–339).
16. Keynes 1973a, p. 340.
17. Ibid., pp. 339–340.
18. The two Robinsons and Kahn argued that: 'For the truth of the proposition that an increase in *I*[nvestment] will lead to an increase in *O*[utput], the two following conditions appear to use to be sufficient, though not necessary: (a) That an increase in *I* will lead *per se* to a rise in the demand for consumption goods … (b) That the conditions of supply of consumption goods are not affected by a change in *I* …' (Keynes 1979, pp. 43–44).
19. Schumpeter 1934, Chapter II.
20. '[S]avings and investment are equal *ex definitione*, whatever interest level exists on the market' (Ohlin 1937).
21. Keynes 1937c.
22. E.g. Asimakopoulos1983. In response to this, Jan Kregel highlighted the autonomy of investment decisions: 'once the money is spent on new investment it all comes back to the capitalist class in the form of profits anyway: it is not the money, it is the investment that is important' (Kregel 1989).
23. Toporowski 2008b.
24. Kalecki 1954, p. 139. Malcolm Sawyer has acutely summarised the connection between investment and the Principle of Increasing Risk as follows: 'The principle of increasing risk is based on the simple proposition that the

greater is a firm's investment relative to its own finance the greater will be the reduction in the entrepreneur's income if the investment is unsuccessful' (Sawyer 1985, p. 103).

25. Toporowski 1995.
26. 'Cartels warding off ruinous competition will earn profits, but for these profits to be realized, investments must be made, since the total profits of capitalists equal the sum of their consumption plus their investments. If cartels can achieve profits while not investing the only reason is the existence of non-cartelized industry, part of whose assets cartels directly or indirectly appropriate. However, if the entire economy were made up of cartels, then obviously they could not achieve large profits without making large investments' (Kalecki 1933a, pp. 160–161).
27. Kalecki 1968b.
28. This can be illustrated as follows. Assuming, initially at least, a closed economy with no government, total saving, S, can be divided into the retained profits of companies, S_c, and household saving, S_h : $S \equiv S_c + S_h$. Total saving in such an economy is also equal to investment, $S = I$, with the direction of causation being from investment to saving, i.e. the amount that firms spend on investment determines how much saving takes place in the economy. Substituting I for S gives: $I = S_c + S_h$. Rearranging this gives an equation for retained profits: $S_c = I - S_h$. This reveals how crucial is household saving, relative to company investment, for corporate liquidity. If investment falls below the level of household saving ($I < S_h$) the net cash flow of companies, after business expenses and payments for capital, is negative. Companies now have to borrow the excess saving from households. This is what Steindl means by enforced indebtedness. With negative retained profits, the companies are now more inclined to reduce investment further. If household saving remains unresponsive to the fall in investment, retained profits will move even further into deficit, and enforced indebtedness will rise further. Conversely, if investment exceeds household saving, then the excess returns to companies as positive retained profits for the sector as a whole. Additional investment may now be undertaken without the need for external financing. More generally, this analysis highlights the importance of appropriate deficit financing by the government so that, if investment falls off, a fiscal deficit removes the excess household investment and 'returns it', as additional expenditure, to the company sector. See Steindl 1982.
29. Steindl 1952, p. 115.
30. Kalecki 1943, p. 86.
31. Steindl 1952, p. 117.
32. Ibid., pp. 118–119.
33. Keynes 1936, p. 84.
34. Hayek 1932.

11. The Kalecki–Steindl theory of financial fragility

This chapter is a contribution to economic methodology, history of economic thought, and the analysis of current financial developments. It shows how economic concepts can be refined and developed beyond their original purpose for use in a better understanding of economic developments with which the original authors of those concepts could not have been familiar. It traces the origins of household saving as a factor in the macroeconomics of Kalecki through to its role in precipitating financial crises. Finally, the chapter shows how in circumstances of asset inflation, the character and significance of household saving changes.

The chapter is structured as follows. Section 11.1 presents the role of household saving in Kalecki's business cycle theory. Section 11.2 shows how Steindl created a theory of financial fragility out of household saving. Section 11.3 shows how asset inflation reduces household saving and thereby shifts financial fragility from the firm sector to the household sector.

11.1 HOUSEHOLD SAVING IN KALECKI'S ANALYSIS

Kalecki's analysis is based on the reproduction (or as we would nowadays call them, circular flow of income) schemes put forward by Marx in Volume II of *Capital*. In his analysis, Marx argued that surplus value is turned into money by the expenditure of capitalists: 'it is the capitalist class itself that throws the money into circulation which serves for the realisation of … surplus value incorporated in … commodities'.[1] Whereas Marx emphasised capitalists' consumption as the way in which capitalists 'realise' their surplus value, Kalecki was able to show that the realisation of profit was chiefly done through capitalists' expenditure on investment, as well as their expenditure on their own consumption.[2] This can be easily shown as follows.

According to the standard national income identity, in any given period, total national income (Y) is equal to consumption (C) plus gross fixed capital expenditure, or investment (I), plus the fiscal deficit, plus the trade surplus.

Saving (S) is then equal to Y – C, which is then equal to investment, plus the fiscal deficit plus the trade surplus. Abstracting away from the fiscal surplus and the trade surplus, and in an economy in which there are only capitalists and workers, saving and consumption can be divided up into the saving and consumption respectively of capitalists and workers:

$$C = C_c + C_w; \text{ and } S = S_c + S_w$$

So that:

$$Y - C = S = S_c + S_w = I \quad (1)$$

The surplus or profits of capitalists (P) is also, by definition, equal to their expenditure on their own consumption (C_c) plus their saving (S_c):

$$P = C_c + S_c$$

Since, by (1) above, capitalist saving is equal to their investment expenditure minus the saving of workers, it follows that $P = C_c + I - S_w$, which can be rearranged to give the familiar Kalecki profits equation:

$$P = I + C_c - S_w \quad (2)$$

In other words, capitalists' profits are equal to their expenditure on fixed capital, plus their expenditure on consumption, minus workers' saving. Of course this is derived from national income identities, so the equation itself cannot yield any causal mechanism. This has to be obtained by a consideration of its economic significance:

> What is the proper meaning of this equation? Does it mean that profits in a certain period determine capitalists' consumption and investment, or the

other way around? The answer to this question depends on which of these items is directly subject to the decisions of capitalists. Now, it is clear that they may decide to consume and invest more in a certain short period than in the preceding period, but they cannot decide to earn more. It is therefore their investment and consumption decisions which determine profits, and not vice versa.[3]

In this analysis, workers' saving clearly has a negative effect on profits. It acts as a 'leakage' whereby money spent by capitalists on wages does not return to capitalists in the form of sales of wage goods. With capitalists' saving, the situation is more complex. Kalecki divides such saving up into 'entrepreneurs' saving' or the undistributed profits of companies, and the saving of 'rentiers', or those who own companies and financial assets. Because of their relatively high and stable incomes (except at times of hyperinflation), rentiers have a high propensity to save, and this saving stays relatively constant. Unlike entrepreneurs' saving, which is used to finance investment and is therefore matched by expenditure, rentiers' saving is a steady 'leakage' of income from the circular flow of money that capitalists put into circulation by their expenditure.

In this analysis, rentiers' and workers' saving is the result of what Marx described as 'a stagnation of circulation', whereas entrepreneurs' saving is 'merely the creation of money capital existing temporarily in latent form and intended to function as productive capital'.[4] With his analysis clearly focused on an investment-driven business cycle, Kalecki incorporated the rentiers' saving as a factor in what he called the 'trend', i.e. the direction of economic growth disregarding 'the pure business cycle'.[5] He argued that such saving tends to give a negative trend. In his last discussion of rentiers' saving, Kalecki merely assumed that it is small in relation to entrepreneurial saving, or retained profits, and that the two types of saving are proportionate to each other.[6] This would tend to make rentiers' saving fluctuate with the profits cycle.

Kalecki's classification of rentiers' saving as a trend factor makes such saving a weak foundation for any theory of financial fragility or crisis. A theory of financial fragility or crisis is by definition an explanation of economic breakdown caused or rooted in the financial system. While financial fragility may take time to build up, its adverse consequences should be apparent in the fluctuation of economic variables, rather than their averages or any trend. It was Josef Steindl, Kalecki's friend and associate, who turned his friend's theory of saving into a theory of financial fragility.

11.2 STEINDL'S THEORY OF FINANCIAL FRAGILITY

Steindl's analysis is more advanced and perhaps more general than that of Kalecki because Steindl looked more broadly at the impact of middle-class saving behaviour on the dynamics of the capitalist economy.[7] The version that is presented here is the one Steindl later put forward.[8]

Consider the Keynesian saving identity, in which saving (S) is the sum of firms' gross fixed capital formation (I), the fiscal deficit (G – T), and the foreign trade surplus (X – M). If we divide up total saving into Household Saving (S_H) and Firms' Saving (S_F), we get the following identity:

$$S \equiv S_H + S_F \equiv I + (G - T) + (X - M) \qquad (3)$$

These are all flow variables over a given period of time. Household saving is broadly related to income. Both Kalecki and Steindl confirmed Hobson's observation that the middle classes and those on higher incomes account for the vast bulk of household saving, for the obvious reason that they have higher incomes than people on lower incomes, and it is easier to save out of higher income.

In the theory of saving, household saving is the residual income of households that is not consumed. In the case of firms, their saving is the residual profit that they have, after their expenditure on the costs of producing their goods and services, and after payment of income commitments to holders of their financial liabilities (i.e. creditors, and holders of equity). In other words, firms' saving is the retained profits of all firms in the economy, or what Kalecki called 'entrepreneurs' saving'.

Firms' saving plays a crucial part in the dynamics of the capitalist economy. The vast bulk of capital accumulation by firms is financed out of retained profits. This was first noted by Kalecki, and was confirmed in studies by Locke Anderson, Victoria Chick and by recent research that I have done with Marilyn Polena.[9] Through its influence on capital expenditure, firm saving is a crucial factor in capitalist dynamics, i.e. inflation, employment and business fluctuations.

This is apparent if equation (1) is re-arranged to give:

$$S_F \equiv I - S_H + (G - T) + (X - M) \qquad (4)$$

Once again, for the sake of simplicity, the sum of the fiscal deficit and the trade surplus is disregarded. This yields an identity in which firms' retained profits (S_F) are equal to their gross capital expenditure minus household saving.

An implication of this is the Keynesian formulation that Investment determines Saving. The Steindl formulation given above retains Kalecki's insight that investment determines the retained profits of firms. However, household saving is a financial barrier to retained profits: Firms will only end up with retained profits amounting to the difference between firms' investment and household saving. If household saving exceeds the level of investment, then firms' saving becomes a net financial deficit. In this way, saving at all times equals investment. But the factor which equalises

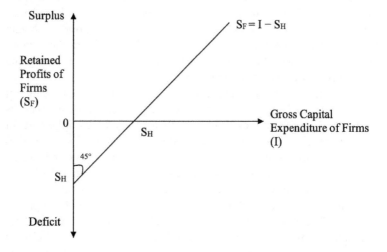

Figure 11.1   Household saving and firms' retained profits in industrial capitalism

Note: Saving = Firms' saving (S_F) + Household Saving (S_H) = Gross Capital Expenditure of Firms (I)

them in practice is not the rate of interest, as most textbooks teach, but the net retained profits or financial deficit of the business sector. This is illustrated in Figure 11.1.

The figure shows the dependence of firms' net cash flow (retained profits – the curve S_F in the diagram) on investment and the level of household saving. On the vertical axis is shown the net financial surplus or deficit of the company sector. On the horizontal axis is shown the level of gross investment in the economy. S_H marks the threshold level of investment that investment must reach if the company sector as a whole is to avoid going into deficit. If investment exceeds that threshold, then firms receive a net cash inflow. If investment falls below the level of household saving, firms as a whole experience a financial deficit.

In Steindl, this relationship between household saving and the financial surpluses or deficits of firms plays a key part in the business cycle. If investment falls below the level of household saving, firms find themselves paying out more in costs, and payments to holders of their financial obligations, than they receive in income. Firms will then borrow to make up the deficit, and the rise in their indebtedness will tend to reduce investment further. Kalecki had argued that this is caused by the 'inelasticity of saving' with respect to investment.[10] In other words, when investment falls, this does not immediately affect the incomes of recipients of higher incomes who account for the bulk of saving. Their continued saving prevents the money that firms throw into circulation, in the process of production, from returning to firms as sales revenue equal or greater than their costs of production and financing. In order to cope with this unexpected financial deficit firms continue to reduce their investment, driving the economy into recession, until household saving falls below the level of investment.

In his pioneering study *Maturity and Stagnation in American Capitalism* Josef Steindl gave a more detailed account of household saving, and showed that it was largely accounted for by rentier incomes, and the incomes of the middle classes.[11] Rentier incomes are largely received through the intermediation of banks and financial institutions, which stabilise those incomes through diversification. The saving of rentiers is therefore largely unaffected by a rise in the financial deficit of firms. Some humbler investors whose wealth does not allow them to diversify their portfolios, may find their incomes affected by the financial difficulties of firms. But such investors are marginal in economic and saving terms.

The remainder of household saving is accounted for by the saving of the middle classes, i.e. those employed in public administration, education, the liberal professions and, increasingly today, the managerial bureaucracy engaged in the administration of financial, industrial and commercial corporations. This social group is largely disconnected from the industrial business cycle, which does not affect those working in public administration, education and the liberal professions. Even the management of financial, industrial and commercial corporations may, if those corporations are large enough, insulate their incomes from industrial fluctuations by diversifying the business of those corporations.

This high and stable level of middle-class saving forms a threshold that forces firms into unanticipated debt, when their gross capital expenditure approaches that threshold, and then falls below it. Firms respond to such 'enforced indebtedness' by postponing investment (it is much more difficult to reduce the costs of current production) and using the money saved to repay debts. This merely prolongs the industrial crisis, because it reduces investment even more below the household saving threshold. Investment is then further reduced. The crisis continues until public sector projects or replacement investment (depreciation) induces a rise in investment.

This prolonged industrial crisis is typical of the difficulties that affected industries in Britain and the United States in the 1950s and the 1960s. At the time, these difficulties were attributed to a lack of competitiveness against industrial producers in East Asia, the greed of trade unions and so on. But the true cause of these crises was the thrift of the middle classes, with memories of their difficulties in the Great Depression, and the unequal distribution of income. The situation was made worse in the United States by that country's greater inequality. As Kalecki observed, '"the rich are richer" in the USA than in the UK' and therefore save more.[12]

11.3   THE THEORY OF ASSET PRICE INFLATION

The situation changed in the 1970s with developments that laid the basis for a new financial cycle. The proliferation of unregulated credit (most notably in the Euro-markets) and the ease with which credit can be expanded against rising collateral values, undermined financial regulation and created a new spirit of competition and innovation in banking and financial markets. Legislation greatly expanded the scope of funded pension schemes, in part at least on the grounds that this would direct more finance into industrial investment and thereby revive the industrial fortunes of the United Kingdom and the United States. As we now know, the industrial revival did not happen, for reasons outlined below. But the inflow of money into pension funds and its placement in financial securities set off a prolonged financial boom. At the same time, the removal of restrictions on housing credit inflated house prices.

With the expansion of the financial markets, and their influence on economic activity beyond merely financing trade and investment, a new phase of capitalist development has emerged in which companies and households have their economic activities increasingly determined by development in capital and asset markets. The mechanics of asset price inflation has been analysed elsewhere as the theory of capital market inflation.[13] This section discusses the impact on economic dynamics of this new development. As a preliminary, it is useful to review the market processes that operate in capital markets. Similar processes occur in the market for housing that has more relevance for more households than the processes in capital markets that affect also companies and financial intermediaries.

Capital markets, i.e. markets for financial assets, do not fix prices that make supply equal to demand, except in a notional sense. Financial markets typically operate for extended periods out of equilibrium. When the demand for financial securities exceeds the amount of money that holders and issuers of those securities are prepared to take out of the market, prices rise. As prices rise, demand for those assets, far from falling off, is enhanced by a speculative demand for assets to benefit from capital gains. However, prices of securities do not rise equally across all markets. Short-term securities and bonds usually have the price at which they are repaid written into the terms of the bond. As the date of their repayment approaches, their market price converges on their repayment price. The market price of such bonds will only exceed that repayment price by a small margin reflecting any differences between the interest payable on such a bond, and the interest payable on equivalent new issues. Excess demand for new securities will therefore inflate most of all equities (common stocks) that do not have any guaranteed repayment value.

Asset and capital market inflation allow debts to be written off against capital gains. The mechanism for such write-offs works only as long as the credit system is fuelling more credit into the market to facilitate the asset sales used to repay debts. When that stops, the liquidity of the market collapses and debt deflation sets in. The dependence of capital gains on net credit inflows into a given asset market turns the whole market into a Ponzi scheme (see Chapter 14 below). Financial fragility in such markets arises because, while the market may need net credit inflows to sustain a given rate of capital gain, there is no mechanism to ensure that sufficient credit will automatically flow into the market to more than offset the credit being taken out of the market to write off debts and finance other activities. If capital gains cannot be realised, then the whole mechanism for writing off debts against capital gains breaks down.

The majority of securities are issued by financial intermediaries and bought by other financial intermediaries ('in an era of finance, finance mostly finances finance'). This issue therefore does not constitute any net expansion of credit, or of the balance sheets of non-financial businesses, such as would take out of the markets any excess net inflow of money into those markets. The non-financial sectors that do take money out of the markets are governments, and corporations. The finance that governments take out of the markets is limited by their fiscal position (the balance between government income and expenditure). An excess demand for securities, such as was set off by the inauguration of funded pension schemes in the United Kingdom and the United States, therefore impacts most directly on the balance sheet operations of corporations. During the 1980s, corporations that issued securities in the capital markets found that they could issue shares cheaply. In particular, with capital market inflation, shares came to be held not just for the sake of their dividend income, which is paid by the company, but also for capital gains, which are not paid by the company but by other buyers in the market for the shares.

As a result of the excess demand for shares, corporations have issued capital in excess of what they need to finance their commercial and industrial operations. In the past the over-capitalisation of companies might have been avoided because it would have involved the 'watering down' of profits (sharing a given amount of profits among more shareholders), or loss of control by the directors of a company who could no longer control the majority of shares at a company general meeting. However, today's shareholders are mostly institutions whose large diversified portfolios are sub-contracted to professional fund managers and rated on financial returns, rather than on their active running of companies. By and large they have too many diverse holdings to take any other than a financial interest in a company. At the same time, new techniques of senior management remuneration have tended to replace profit-related pay with share price-related pay, through stock options. Along with new techniques of debt management, stock option remuneration has removed inhibitions about the over-capitalisation of companies.

Additional capital raised has been used to replace bank borrowing with cheaper long-term capital. Replacing borrowing with shares also has the advantage that pre-tax profits can be made to rise by the reduction in interest cost. Where excess capital has not been used to reduce debt, it has been used to buy short-term financial assets. Alternatively, excess capital is committed to buying and selling companies. This accelerates the turnover of credit in the capital market, further pushing up the price of stocks. Hence the extended festival of merger and takeover activity and balance sheet restructuring that has characterised corporate finance since the 1980s.

One may wonder what happened to the hopes of industrial revival, entertained at the end of the 1970s, when it was argued that funded pension schemes would make more long-term capital available for industrial investment. These hopes have by and large not materialised. Britain and the United States, where capital market inflation has been most heavily promoted, remain economies with weak industrial investment and performance, for which the cause is fairly obvious to anyone who has followed recent changes in corporate finance. Large corporations, which account for the vast bulk of private sector investment, now have excess capital and engage more in balance sheet restructuring (buying and selling financial assets; issuing and repaying liabilities). Such restructuring leaves corporations with larger risky financial market exposures, which therefore require the holding of greater amounts of liquid assets (short-term deposits, holding of securities). If a company finds itself with too many liquid assets, profits can be immediately increased by using the excess liquid assets to repay debt. Indeed, this is a far more certain way of raising profits than the prolonged and uncertain business of investment in plant and equipment. Industrial regeneration is a dream of engineers, from which companies are awoken by their finance directors to face the irrefutable realities of balance sheet restructuring as the only financially viable way forward for all companies.

The overall effect of company over-capitalisation on banks has been to make banks more fragile. Before the 1970s, the largest, most reliable borrowers from banks were large corporations. From the end of the 1970s, such corporations found that they could borrow much more cheaply by issuing their own bills (company paper) or directly from the inter-bank market. If banks want to hold company loans, they have to buy them in the market at yields that give banks no profit over their cost of funds in the capital or money markets. The loss of their best customers has turned banks towards fee-related business in derivatives and debt obligations markets, and towards lending into the property market and to other risky customers that banks had hitherto treated with much more caution. The overall effect, from the savings and loans scandals of the early 1980s, to the sub-prime market crisis since 2007, has clearly been to make banking markets much more fragile.

The rise in the value of their real estate and financial assets has induced a change in saving behaviour of the middle classes. Hitherto the middle classes saved more or less passively, along lines loosely related to the Life Cycle Saving Hypothesis, or the New Classical consumption function: Income was put into savings to support future consumption in retirement. Only among the small minority of the wealthy upper classes was wealth used as a substitute for income, with legacies and realised wealth being used to support current expenditure. From the 1980s onwards, active use of their balance sheets to generate cash flow became much more common among the middle classes. Asset inflation in the housing market allowed the emergence of an alternative 'welfare state of the middle classes' based on issuing financial liabilities against rising asset values, or the sale of inflated assets. Private health care, fees for education, and replacement income in periods of unemployment, have increasingly, among the middle classes, been accommodated by borrowing against wealth whose value has conveniently been rising much faster than current expenditure, or selling such wealth.

When assets are no longer largely held long-term, to be realised only on death or retirement, but come to be held more briefly, for capital gain purposes, their turnover inevitably increases. The more common use of debt or asset sales to pay for current expenditure has brought down saving rates in the household sectors of the United States and Great Britain to negligible or negative levels.[14] This in turn has removed the household saving threshold which firms' investment must exceed in order to provide the business sector as a whole with a financial surplus. Now the total amount of firms' capital expenditure is realised as net cash flow in the form of retained profits. This is illustrated in Figure 11.2.

The business cycle is now different. Industrial crises no longer play a part in bringing economic booms to an end. Such crises are largely eliminated by the over-capitalisation of corporations, which makes it easier for corporations to maintain their liquidity. Industrial crises have now been replaced by a less dramatic under-investment in fixed capital by those companies. Booms are increasingly driven by middle-class consumption, sustained by capital gains extracted from inflating asset markets. The end of a boom is marked by a financial rather than industrial

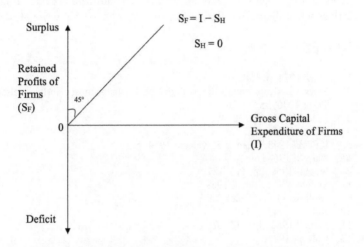

Figure 11.2   Household saving and firms' retained profits in financialised capitalism

crisis. But the resilience of consumption, which in wealthy countries remains one of the most stable elements of total expenditure, ensures that economic recessions are weak.

11.4   CONCLUSION

This chapter has argued that asset and capital market inflation has brought about a relative economic stability by removing the 'congestion' to the circular flow of income induced by household saving. It has not considered the consequences of the decline of industry in the financialised economies, with manufacturing being the main industrial casualty of financial inflation. Nor has this chapter considered the extent to which financial inflation in the United States and the United Kingdom, by backing their currencies with inflated asset values, has accommodated the macroeconomic imbalances that have resulted from a weakening industrial performance in those countries. Essential to the theory of financial fragility is the idea that macroeconomic imbalances do not work themselves out in some reified way, abstracted from, or a mere conjuncture of prices in, the economic calculations of 'economic agents'. In a credit-based capitalist economy, such imbalances are resolved through the constraints that debts impose upon firms and households. The ultimate financial fragility arrives when financial inflation can no longer be used to write off debt.

NOTES

1. Marx 1974, p. 338.
2. Marx's analysis, and its link with that of Kalecki is most clearly discussed in Trigg 2006, pp. 22–28.
3. Kalecki 1943, pp. 48–49.
4. Marx 1974, p. 353.
5. Kalecki 1943, Chapter 5; Kalecki 1954, p. 159.
6. Kalecki 1968a.
7. Steindl 1952, pp. 113–121.
8. Steindl 1982; Steindl 1989.
9. Anderson 1964; Chick 1993.
10. Kalecki 1943, p. 86.
11. Steindl 1952, pp. 113–121.
12. Kalecki 1945.
13. Toporowski 1993a, Chapter 3; Toporowski 2000, part 1.
14. The data on this is distorted by the inclusion of much small business debt into the household sector. This arises because many, possibly most, owners of unincorporated businesses finance those business through household borrowing. This has led many 'financialisation' theorists to conclude that corporations with liquid assets are indebting households, whereas in reality they are indebting smaller businesses.

PART IV

Critical theories of finance in the twentieth century: the financial instability hypothesis

12. The monetary theory of Kalecki and Minsky

The monetary theory of Michał Kalecki and Hyman P. Minsky is usually placed within the post-Keynesian monetary tradition.[1] By monetary theory is meant here the way in which money circulates in a financially sophisticated capitalist economy, rather than a universal account of the attributes of money. Money is a social artefact and any account of it necessarily relative to historical circumstances.

This chapter does not present a comprehensive account of post-Keynesian monetary theory, or of German monetary theory, or even the monetary theories of Keynes, Kalecki or Minsky. Hence the rather summary treatment of German and post-Keynesian theories. Rather the chapter highlights particular differences between the monetary theories of Kalecki and Minsky, and post-Keynesian monetary theory, and particular similarities between the monetary theories of these two individuals and German monetary theory.

The post-Keynesian view derives from the work of John Maynard Keynes, with the important modification that money is assumed to be endogenous, a view at variance with the view held by Keynes up to the *General Theory* and beyond (see below), where money and bank credit is set by the central bank (and hence exogenous). The endogenous view, according to which the demand for credit determines its supply, was subsequently revived by Nicholas Kaldor and later post-Keynesians such as Paul Davidson, Basil Moore, Victoria Chick and Sheila Dow in their well-known works.

The theory of monetary endogeneity locates the agency determining the supply and demand for money in the banking system. The Keynesian tradition places this in the money market in which commercial banks confront the central bank, as the supplier of money, with their demand for central bank money to hold as reserves or convert into bank-notes for withdrawal into circulation. Post-Keynesian monetary theory emphasises the mechanisms within the banking system that make it responsive to what Keynes referred to as 'the fringe of unsatisfied borrowers'.

According to Keynes this fringe allowed the banking system to ration credit by means other than the rate of interest:

> The existence of this unsatisfied fringe and of a variability in the banks' stand-ards of eligibility of borrowers in respects other than the rate of interest allows the Banking System a means of influencing the rate of interest supplementary to mere changes in the short-term rate of interest ... the Bank of England does not fix bank-rate and leave the quantity of bank-money to find its own level; nor does it fix the quantity of bank-money and leave the bank-rate to find its own level. It fixes *both* – and fixes them, to a certain extent independently.[2]

Among post-Keynesians from Kaldor onwards, this central bank control over the amount of bank credit is denied and replaced by the notion that the demand for bank-money or credit is itself determined by the rate of interest and uncertainty that govern the real investment for which credit is required. This is to some degree justified by 'revolving fund of finance' arguments from Keynes: money loaned by banks for investment becomes available for lending out again, so that successive tranches of investment may be undertaken without the need for expanding the supply of credit.[3] This view, for example, modifies the 'loanable funds' plus uncertainty interpretation that Asimakopoulos gives to the post-Keynesian relation-ship between credit and investment, into which he incorporates Kalecki,[4] or the passive lending that Jan Kregel sees in Kalecki's theory:

> In simple terms, Kalecki assumes that whenever individual capitalists are inclined to spend in excess of their budget constraints in order to invest, the bank oblige by creating the appropriate amounts of commercial bank credits.[5]

This chapter presents a different view of Kalecki's monetary theory. This is most obvious at the point at which investment, or the process of capital accumulation, is articulated with this theory. In the first place, Kalecki emphasised the priority that firms give to financing investment out of retained profits.[6] Furthermore, Kalecki also argued that investment spending generates profits, in the form of accumulations of bank deposits in the accounts of capitalists.[7] This is a 'macroeconomic' circuit by which bank lending results in bank deposits. It may be contrasted with the purely banking circuit implicit in the balance sheet identity that means that a bank loan is a bank deposit awaiting use as means of payment, or

Keynes's 'revolving fund of finance' in which bank loans return to them not as deposits, but as loan repayments:

> If investment is proceeding at a steady rate, the finance (or the commitments to finance) required can be supplied from a revolving fund of a more or less constant amount, one entrepreneur having his finance replenished for the purpose of a projected investment as another exhausts his on paying for his completed investment.[8]

The same two mechanisms articulating retained profits with bank loans for investment, and then investment resulting in profits, through a 'macroeconomic' circuit, may also be found in Minsky.[9] The macroeconomic circuit is descended from German monetary theory, rather than the 'medium of exchange' cum money market analysis of Alfred Marshall, from which Keynes built his theory. It is therefore useful, or at least provides some economy of intellectual effort, to consider the roots of the monetary analysis of both Minsky and Kalecki in German monetary theory. In the section that follows, the key features of German monetary theory that influenced Kalecki and Minsky are outlined. This is then followed by a section explaining how Kalecki was brought into the German monetary tradition, and what elements of his work reflect that tradition. In the final section a similar interpretation of Minsky is provided. The chapter concludes by reflecting on some of the implications of their work for economic policy in general, and monetary policy in particular.

12.1 GERMAN MONETARY THEORY (SCANDALOUSLY ABBREVIATED)

German monetary theory is a complex of competing doctrines and methodologies.[10] It includes, for example, an Austrian stream, associated with the work of Mises and Hayek. This stressed convertibility with gold as a regulator of money and credit. But there was another stream, emanating from the work of Knut Wicksell. His *Interest and Prices*, published in Swedish in 1898, was based on an extensive study of English monetary theory, including the Banking School. He also appears to have studied the economic reproduction schemes of Marx, from Volume II of *Capital*.[11] Among the seminal ideas that Wicksell advanced was the idea of a credit cycle, driven by differences between the money rate of interest and the 'natural' rate of interest, the latter being the marginal product of capital. But he took from Marx the idea that the capitalist economy is a system in which money spent circulates in the economy, so that the spending of capitalists on investment and their own consumption comes back to capitalists as profits through the process of production and exchange. Finally, Wicksell put forward the idea of a 'pure credit' economy. In the recent work of Michael Woodford, a 'pure credit' economy has come to mean one in which the money supply is strictly endogenous, to the point where illiquidity is impossible (because additional credit can, by assumption, always be obtained). However, Wicksell's 'pure credit' economy is one in which credit serves as a means of payment, and credit is unconstrained by bank reserves. This is a much better description of twenty-first century banking in the financially advanced countries, than that of Woodford, if only because Wicksell's concept does not exclude all those issues of insolvency and illiquidity that have come to trouble us today.

German monetary theory was carried over into monetary theoretical discussions in the English language by Hayek, Schumpeter and Neisser, only to be overtaken in those discussions by the monetary analysis of Keynes. All three German monetary theorists absorbed the apparently paradoxical proposition of Hartley Withers, that loans create deposits, rather than the other way around, as conventional credit multiplier theory proposes.[12] In other words, the balance sheet of the banking system is not determined by the deposits that are placed in banks, but by the loans that banks advance to their customers. These then appear as additional deposits of customers from whom borrowers buy goods, services and assets with the loans that they have received.

12.2　KALECKI'S MONETARY THEORY

The earliest influence on Kalecki's monetary theory was Hilferding's *Finance Capital*. This work highlights the role of banks in the process of regulating corporate finance and managing markets (the Marxian 'concentration and centralisation of capital' by banks). However, Hilferding did not consider the principle of banking reflux, which underlies Withers-type processes of monetary endogeneity. Kalecki seems to have worked it out himself in developing his ideas on corporate liquidity and investment over the course of the business cycle. An early indicator of his thinking occurs in an essay on 'Inflation and War' (*Inflacja a Wojna*) which he wrote under the pseudonym Henryk Braun for a socialist periodical, the *Socialist Review* (*Przegląd Socjalistyczny*). Here he argued that credit policy could not revive business activity depressed by inadequate demand in the economy. Cheaper and more easily available bank loans, due to 'a more liberal supply of credit by the central bank', would only be taken out in order to pay off existing, more expensive business loans: 'New credits will be used to pay back the old ones and the surprised creditors will bring their repaid credits back to banks thus neatly closing the circle.'[13]

By then Kalecki was already working with the monetary economist who was to have the biggest influence on him, Marek Breit. Breit's early work, before he met Kalecki, was concerned with the scope and significance of interest rate policy in Poland, and displays an extensive knowledge of German monetary theory. At that time, he leaned towards the ideas of Mises and Albert Hahn. Both Mises and Hahn were preoccupied with the inflationary potential of excessive credit creation. Under the influence of Kalecki, and the Depression of the 1930s, Breit moved to a more sceptical view of credit policy which emphasised the expenditure decision of the capitalist firm as the key moment in mobilising credit, rather than the lending decision of the bank (which predominates most notably in New Keynesian credit theory).[14] This principle underlies the Principle of Increasing Risk that Kalecki made into the core of his theory of the firm and integrates his analysis of corporate finance with his theory of investment.[15]

The final link in the reflux of bank lending to bank deposits appears in Kalecki's work in the form of his theory of profits. Here he argued that firms' expenditure on investment returned to them, more or less (depending on the amount of household saving, the fiscal balance, and payments on the foreign trade and capital accounts) as profits:

> [I]f some capitalists increase their investment by using for this purpose their liquid reserves, the profits of other capitalists will rise *pro tanto* and thus the liquid reserves will pass into the possession of the latter. If additional investment is financed by bank credit, the spending of the amounts in question will cause equal amounts of saved profits to accumulate as bank deposits.[16]

Money is intrinsic to Kalecki's (and Keynes's) theory of profits. This may appear strange to theorists who have been bought up over generations to regard the theory of distribution (the determination of profits) as being separate from monetary theory. But the link between them is made clear in the pretext for Rosa Luxemburg's dispute with orthodox Marxists and under-consumptionists who cling to an exploitation theory of profits. Capitalists' profit maximisation is a desire for profits in the form of money, not for profits in the form of labour time or commodities in excess of those paid as wages to workers:

> Reproduction, for its part, can obviously be only resumed when the products of the previous period, the commodities, have been realised; that is converted into money; for capital in the form of money, in the form of pure value, must always be the starting point of reproduction in a capitalist system. The first condition of reproduction for the capitalist producer is thus seen to be a successful realisation of the commodities produced during the previous period of production.[17]

Implicit in this was Kalecki's definition of the capitalist not just as the owner of means of production, but as the owner of money capital that he could use to buy the raw materials and labour for the purposes of production:

> Many economists assume, at least in their abstract theories, a state of business democracy where anybody endowed with entrepreneurial ability can obtain capital for starting a business venture. This picture of the activities of the 'pure' entrepreneur is, to put it mildly, unrealistic. The most important prerequisite for becoming an entrepreneur is the *ownership* of capital.[18]

By 'capital' Kalecki clearly meant *money* capital, rather than titles of ownership of valuable productive equipment. From this passage, Kalecki went on to the key implication of this ownership of money capital for economic activity: 'The above considerations are of great importance for the theory of the determination of investment. One of the important factors of investment decisions is the accumulation of firms' capital out of current profits.'[19]

Kalecki's earliest exposition of his business cycle theory originally contained a section on the monetary mechanisms behind his model of the business cycle entitled 'The Money Market'. This shows a process of investment financing in which capitalists, because of their ownership of money capital, do not even need to borrow money to undertake investments. They simply transfer funds from their reserve accounts to their payment, or current accounts, so that business cycles can occur without any change in the overall size of the balance sheet of the banking system. What does change over the business cycle is the velocity of circulation of bank payment accounts. During an investment boom money is transferred from (inactive) reserve accounts to (active) payment accounts in a boom, and then between payment accounts, during an investment boom. During a recession, the process is reversed with money being transferred from payment accounts into reserves, and a falling away of transfers between payment accounts.[20]

12.3   THE MONETARY THEORY OF MINSKY

The link with German monetary theory is much more obvious in the case of Minsky. The supervisor of his PhD dissertation was Schumpeter, until he died. Minsky's doctoral thesis was a critique of the accelerator principle as an element of the business cycle, arguing that it depended on the indebtedness of capitalist firms.[21] Minsky later investigated the circulation of money in a sophisticated financial capitalist economy for a research study into private capital markets, commissioned by the Commission on Money and Credit, financed by the Ford and Merrill Foundations. Minsky contributed to this a study entitled 'Financial Crisis, Financial Systems and the Performance of the Economy'.[22]

Minsky's study divided money flows into three 'transaction types'. These were flows on 'balance sheet account, income account, and portfolio account'.[23] The 'balance sheet account' consists of those flows that are necessary to maintain existing balance sheets, that is, payments on existing financial liabilities, or from existing assets. These include all 'contractual dated payments of interest, rent, etc., and the payment of dividends …'. The 'income account' consists of money flows being exchanged for goods and services in the economy. Here Minsky added 'it is a matter of research strategy whether all inter-firm payments, or only those related to the purchase of final goods and services – the production of gross national product – should be included'.[24] Finally, portfolio payments are the money flows due to the exchange of either existing assets or newly created financial assets. These he proposed to integrate into what we would now call the 'flow of funds' accounts, showing the evolution of money in circulation and portfolio balances. This analysis of money flows is a key and original feature of the study, which provides an early version of what came to be his 'financial instability hypothesis'.

Minsky seems to have had difficulty in knowing where to place intra-firm money payments in respect of business payments for materials, components, and semi-finished products. After excluding such payments from his analysis he noted: 'It is quite clear that the analysis put forth here would tend to a "Fisherish" concept of transaction velocity rather than a "Marshallian" income, or income and wealth velocity. As a result the firm business to business payments of input-output analysis should be included in any money flows accounting system.'[25] The 'Fisherish' reference is to Fisher's paper 'The Debt Deflation Theory of Great Depressions', a work that Minsky revered. In that paper, Fisher advanced the idea that a capitalist economy that uses credit has two market systems. The first is the well-known system of markets and prices for goods in current production that is the staple of microeconomic theory. The second is the credit system, in which monetary and financial assets are exchanged, giving rise to future payment obligations or receipts.[26] The distinction forms the basis for Minsky's theory of financial crisis. It also contrasts with Kalecki's theory. Whereas Kalecki had argued that an investment boom was possible without any increase in business borrowing (see previous section), Fisher's and Minsky's analyses introduce finance as a factor in economic crisis through the increase in debt-financed investment in the course of the economic boom.

This analysis turns out to be somewhat similar to that advanced by the German monetary theorist and Marxist Hans Neisser (of whom Keynes wrote 'I find Dr. Neisser's general attitude to monetary problems particularly sympathetic, and am hopeful he may feel the same about my work'[27]). In his 1928 book *Der Tauschwert des Geldes* (The Exchange Value of Money) Neisser had divided up cash balances into 'balance reserves', held against contingencies by producers and consumers, and the 'operating funds' to meet regular shortfalls of income against expenditure. To these Neisser attributed different velocities of circulation.[28] In a strange anticipated query of Minsky's remarks about business to business payments, the writer on German monetary theory Howard Ellis had doubts too about Neisser's and Hayek's inclusion of inter-firm payments for materials, components, and semi-finished products. These payments would increase with firm specialisation, and so are an unstable foundation for any monetary theory relying on stable velocities of circulation.[29]

Minsky went on, from the late 1970s onwards, to adopt the Kalecki profits theory, according to which investment in a given period yields, in that same period, profits for firms. This appears in his most important work *Stabilizing an Unstable Economy*.[30] However, he did not draw the monetary conclusion from this theory, namely that loan-financed investment adds to firms' bank deposits in the form of retained profits.[31]

12.4 CONCLUSION

Both Kalecki and Minsky derived their monetary economics from the German discussions during the first third of the last century. This led them to the conclusion that the expenditure of capitalists determines the circulation of money in the economy, and credit or monetary policy only affects the balance sheet of the banking system. This is a fundamentally different view from that of Keynes and the post-Keynesians, who argued and continue to argue that credit or monetary policy determines the circulation of money in the economy (except in the unlikely case of a 'liquidity trap') through its impact on the expenditure of capitalist firms. In the case of Keynes and the post-Keynesians, such expenditure draws down the liquidity of bank balance sheets, but does not expand those balance sheets. Most economists today have forgotten, if they ever learned, the conclusion of Withers, that loans create deposits or, in the version of Kalecki and partially that of Minsky, that loan-financed investment expenditure creates its own profits and equivalent income deposits in the banking system.[32] This link between capitalists' expenditure and bank credit forms the common theoretical connection between German monetary theory and modern circuit theory of money.[33]

NOTES

1. See Sawyer 1985, Chapter 5; Sawyer 2001; Wray 1990, 2010.
2. Keynes 1930, pp. 365–366.
3. Keynes 1937b, pp. 208–209.
4. Asimakopoulos 1983.
5. Kregel 1989.
6. Anderson 1964; Kalecki 1954, Chapter 9.
7. Kalecki 1954, p. 50.
8. Keynes 1937b, p. 209.
9. Minsky 1954, 1986.
10. Ellis 1934; Bellofiore 2015.
11. Wicksell 1935, p. 13.
12. Withers 1909. See also Chick 1986.
13. Kalecki 1932.
14. Breit 1933, 1935b; Kowalik 1992, pp. 239–243.
15. Breit 1935b; Kalecki 1954, Chapter 8.
16. Kalecki 1954, p. 50.
17. Luxemburg 1951, pp. 39–40.
18. Kalecki 1954, pp. 94–95.
19. Ibid., p. 95.
20. Kalecki 1933/1990, pp. 93–98.
21. Minsky 1954/2004.
22. Minsky 1964.
23. Ibid., pp. 233–235.
24. Ibid., p. 234.
25. Ibid., p. 235.
26. Fisher 1933.

27. Keynes 1930, p. 197.
28. Neisser 1928.
29. Ellis 1934, pp. 174–175.
30. Minsky 1986, Chapter 8.
31. Lavoie and Seccareccia 2001; Toporowski 2010.
32. Toporowski 2012.
33. Bellofiore 1989; Halevi and Taouil 2002.

13. From money to Minsky: Henry Simons

The origins of Minsky's ideas in the work of John Maynard Keynes, and Minsky's own rather idiosyncratic interpretation of Keynes are well known. Keynes was the subject of Minsky's first book-length work after his PhD thesis.[1] In that thesis, Minsky made relatively few references to Keynes, and they are mainly the predictable ones: Keynes on uncertainty, consumption, liquidity preference and the liquidity trap.[2] All of these refer to the *General Theory*, and none show the insights into Keynes's work that were to be developed in that first book, Minsky's *John Maynard Keynes*.[3] In that doctoral thesis, another later influence, the Polish business cycle theorist Michał Kalecki, has his Principle of Increasing Risk correctly cited as a theory of the size of firms. However, Kalecki's internal finance constraint on investment, which came to have a central role in Minsky's analysis after he returned in 1970 from his year in Cambridge, UK, is mistakenly attributed to the monetary business theorist Ralph Hawtrey following a citation from the econometrician Sho-Chieh Tsiang.[4] However, the economist who arguably directed Minsky towards the macroeconomics of financial disturbance, the Chicago liberal Henry Simons, is not mentioned at all in Minsky's doctoral thesis.

This is a most surprising omission. Simons had taught Minsky at Chicago. In his later memoir of his Chicago years, published in the *Banca Nazionale del Lavoro Quarterly Review* in 1986, Minsky recalled the very personal relationship that he had with Simons. It was Simons who introduced Minsky to the idea that the financial system in the United States was structurally flawed and who explained how the banking system had contributed to the Great Depression, without resorting to tales about incorrect monetary policy, or imbalances between saving and investment. When Minsky finished his military service in 1946, he was offered a generous fellowship to return to Chicago, but turned it down for a less lucrative studentship at Harvard. His reason was that the three economists whom he most admired at Chicago were no longer there:

Viner had gone to Princeton; Lange, whose socialist commitment had inspired Minsky to study economics had, to Minsky's disgust, thrown in his lot with the Polish Communists; and Simons was dead.[5] Simons, who was prone to melancholy, had according to legend committed suicide in despair at the onset of Keynesianism. Six years before he wrote his memoir, in his Preface to his 1982 volume of essays, Minsky had mentioned Simons even ahead of Lange and Schumpeter, as an influence: 'As a student, I was most influenced by Henry C. Simons, Oscar Lange, and Josef Schumpeter'.[6]

13.1 SIMONS AND BANKING REFORM

Simons deserves consideration not only because Minsky appears so inexplicably to have omitted him from his thesis. Such consideration is further justified because many of those who have heard of him today know him from the very partial account of his work given by Milton Friedman. Hayek was later to suggest that Simons shared Hawtrey's views on the monetary business cycle (see below), and there is no doubt that Simons was a theorist of critical finance in the special sense that he argued that the real economy is vulnerable to crises emanating from the financial system.[7] But, whereas Hawtrey stressed the natural instability of credit as a factor in business cycles, Simons argued that the structure of the financial system was a key factor in exacerbating disequilibrium in the non-financial sector of the economy. In his classic article 'Rules versus Authorities in Monetary Policy' published in the *Journal of Political Economy* in 1936, the later late-twentieth-century discussion on central bank independence appears turned on its head. Simons argued that the regulation of liquidity in the financial system necessitates the absorption of central banking into the Treasury (finance ministry) function of the government.

Sensible to the financial debauchery and collapse of the first four decades of the twentieth century in the United States, Simons was a strong critic of the kind of financial entrepreneurship that Minsky later also criticised. Simons believed that such entrepreneurship was the result of liberal banking policies that encouraged excessive credit and discouraged investment by requiring business to keep liquidity tied up against a possible inability to roll over short-term loans. Simons concluded that financial intermediation needs to be subject to strict rules, and that the fiscal authorities need to have discretion over monetary policy in order to be able to regulate credit. This discretion had to be with the fiscal authorities because their open market operations determine the reserves of the banking system.[8] Simons had even argued for the abolition of central banking, because he believed that its functions are more effectively carried out by government treasuries. The elimination of central banking also followed from his adherence to the doctrine of full reserve (100 per cent reserve) banking. If banks are obliged to hold the equivalent of all their deposits as reserves, then there is clearly no need for provision of reserves by a central bank.[9]

After the publication of his monetary history of the United States, Milton Friedman gave the critical reassessment of Simons referred to above. Friedman argued that Simons had failed to realise the disastrous consequences of the contraction of bank credit in 1930–3, which Friedman revealed in his history. In fact, Simons could not have been unaware of the contraction: Irving Fisher had been arguing much the same around 1933 and both Fisher and Simons were involved in the discussions around the reform of the Federal Reserve System to stabilise the faltering US banking system.[10] However, Friedman drew a conclusion that was directly contrary to that of Simons. In Friedman's view, consistently argued since 1948, the monetary authorities, rather than banks, had to be bound by rules on credit expansion because, according to Friedman, the relationship between reserves and credit is essentially stable.[11] It goes almost without saying that, in the monetarist analysis, the relationship between financial intermediation and the real economy is essentially benign and speculation results from loose monetary policy rather than loose banking. Friedman's claim, that these doctrines were part of the 'oral tradition' of Chicago, had already drawn Patinkin's famous defence of a broader tradition at Chicago.[12]

Simons was therefore the missing link between Hawtrey and Minsky. Hayek hinted at this in criticising Friedman's suggestion that the Great Depression predisposed both Keynes and Simons to fiscal activism. Simons' fiscal schemes were explicitly designed to regulate the liquidity of the financial system, rather than regulating aggregate demand.[13] Hayek wrote to Friedman: 'I believe you are wrong in suggesting that the common element in the doctrines of Simons and Keynes was the influence of the Great Depression. We all held similar ideas in the 1920s. They had been most fully elaborated by R.G. Hawtrey who was all the time talking about the "inherent instability of credit" but he was by no means the only one ...'.[14]

Minsky, like Patinkin, objected to Friedman's narrow interpretation of the Chicago tradition. In a 1969 paper in the *Journal of Finance* Minsky contrasted Simons's view that the '... depression-proof good financial society requires the radical restructuring of the financial system...' with Friedman's view that 'the establishment of the good financial society requires only the adoption of a stable money growth rule by the Federal Reserve System, given that the reform represented by the introduction of deposit insurance had already taken place ... Simons had a financial system rather than a narrow monetary view of the "Banking" problem.'[15]

13.2 MINSKY, SIMONS AND THE STABILITY OF CAPITALISM

An essential difference between Simons and Minsky arises over the question of the inherent stability of capitalism. Simons believed that the capitalist market system was stable and self-adjusting, at least in the sense that a 'largely competitive, free market, free-enterprise system' could be stabilised providing that the government was able to manage the reserves of the banking system and provide sufficient purchasing power in those capitalist markets. In particular, in an article published in 1944, Simons argued that competitive markets were inherently stable. 'General and acute instability is, on any soundly reasoned analysis, primarily attributable to faulty monetary institutions and, in the broadest sense, to unfortunate fiscal policy.'[16] This was prophetic, since it is the fundamental premise of economic and monetary policy in the United States and United Kingdom following the crisis of 2007–8.

The Minsky view was much more radical. Capitalism is unstable not just because of 'faulty monetary institutions' and inappropriate government policy.[17] From the 1970s onwards Minsky attributed instability explicitly to the cyclical shifts in non-financial business investment. Firms indebt themselves in order to finance their investment, and, in rather approximate accordance with Kalecki's theory of profits, investment is necessary to generate the revenues necessary to service debts. The failure of investment to rise sufficiently to provide the financial surpluses necessary to service growing corporate debt gives rise to the financial crisis of which Minsky wrote. His 'financial' crises were therefore industrial crises precipitated by rising indebtedness, rather than bank illiquidity.[18] (In this regard, Minsky overlooked the monetary implication of Kalecki's theory, namely that investment above the level of household saving leads to the accumulation of credit balances on the accounts of non-financial enterprises.[19])

This has important implications for economic policy. Stabilising a banking system without stabilising the industrial and commercial system which those banks serve, leaves the economy still vulnerable to non-financial business fluctuations. Non-financial instability in turn renders financial regulation vulnerable to arguments from bankers and economists to the effect that if only the regulations were made lighter, or even removed altogether, the credit system would automatically alleviate those imbalances, and bring the economy back to equilibrium. And only the ignorant could dismiss such a plea, since we all teach our students that the credit system functions to accommodate economic imbalances and has done so quite effectively for decades with only recent disastrous results. The radical conclusion of Minsky's work ('big bank and big government'[20]) is based on a fundamental insight of business cycle theory, rather than just banking economics, namely that without stabilising the economy at large, banking stabilisation is unlikely to hold. This is an implicit criticism of Minsky's teacher, Simons, for whom the free market in exchange with a stabilised banking system is a guarantee of equilibrium.

Nevertheless, Minsky retained an admiration for Simons and his teacher's belief that the destabilising influence in capitalism is banking rather than, as Chicago later convinced itself, government policy. In his most important and developed exposition of his theory, Minsky declared the writings of Simons, along with Keynes's *General Theory* and Fisher's debt deflation analysis, as providing 'the fundamentals of a theory of financial instability'.[21] He commended Simons's 'serious conservative program of institutional reform and policy operation that remains a model of political economy' and concluded: 'In spite of the passage of fifty years, the substance of Simons' proposals are still worth considering.'[22] Even though Simons's ferocious opposition to Keynesianism repelled Minsky, he still admired the *brio* with which Simons put forward his critique of the American Keynesian Alvin Hansen.[23] This critique, Minsky wrote, 'can be read with pleasure for both its rather unfair attacking style and as a sophisticated attack on the interventionist economy'.[24] The seriousness and sophistication that Minsky found in Simons quite evidently arose because he recognised that Simons had integrated banking and credit into his economic analysis and was prepared to treat it critically, instead of just taking it for granted. For this reason Minsky was prepared to give Simons the critical attention that he gave also to Keynes and Fisher, but which he would not give to Samuelson, Tobin, Hicks or Milton Friedman.

NOTES

1. Minsky 1975.
2. Minsky 1954/2004.
3. Minsky 1975.
4. Minsky 1954/2004, p. 72.
5. Minsky 1988.
6. Minsky 1982b, p. 5.
7. Toporowski 2005, pp. 2–5. Due to pressure to complete my own *Theories of Financial Disturbance* Simons was, unfortunately, omitted from that book.
8. Simons 1936.
9. The discussion around this is perceptively examined by Ronnie J. Phillips in a book, *The Chicago Plan & New Deal Banking Reform*, to which Minsky wrote a Preface (Phillips 1995).
10. Phillips 1995, chapters 3 and 4.
11. Friedman 1967.
12. Patinkin 1961.
13. Simons 1942.
14. Friedman 1967, p. 88.
15. Minsky 1982b, pp. 279, 289.
16. Simons 1944, pp. 107–108.
17. See Vercelli 2001.
18. Minsky 1978.
19. See Steindl 1982; Toporowski 2008a.
20. Minsky 1986.
21. Minsky 1986, p. 172.
22. Minsky 1986, p. 9.
23. Simons 1942.
24. Minsky 1986, p. 122.

14. The financial instability hypothesis

The Financial Instability Hypothesis is the term given by Hyman P. Minsky to his theory explaining why capitalist market economies are prone to instability. The theory integrates macroeconomic analysis with an original microeconomic view of how capitalist firms operate. Financial fragility refers to the build-up of debt that precedes the breakdown in economic activity, in a market capitalist economy with a sophisticated debt-based financial system. The crisis then bequeaths a legacy of unsustainable debt to succeeding periods until a boom revives expenditure and sales revenue sufficiently to make the debt burden manageable, whereupon the cyclical build-up of debt resumes.

The macroeconomic part of the analysis is essentially a business cycle theory in which booms and slumps are driven by business investment in fixed capital. Rising investment causes an increase in general economic activity and sales revenue. Falling investment causes a decline in business activity in general, and a fall in sales revenue. This part of Minsky's analysis was drawn from the work of John Maynard Keynes and his *General Theory*. However, Minsky considered that as investment rose it would become financed by borrowing. The rising debt levels would need to be serviced out of sales revenue, so that if investment, and the resulting sales revenue, fell off, businesses would succumb to a debt crisis. The crisis is then a prelude to economic recession, possibly even a prolonged depression (Minsky was always conscious in his analysis of the possible recurrence of the 1930s Depression through which he had lived in the second decade of his life).

The microeconomic part of the analysis is a highly original approach to economic decision-making in which economic agents (households, banks and firms) make decisions on the basis not just of income and expenditure, as postulated in conventional microeconomic analysis, but also in consideration of their balance sheets. Minsky recognised that, with credit, it is possible to generate cash flow not only from selling commodities, but also from selling assets or entering into debt contracts. A balance sheet therefore represented for Minsky a set of dated financial commitments (liabilities) or claims (assets). The survival of firms therefore depends on the liquidity of those claims and credit availability, as well as the flows of income from which to service those financial commitments.

The liabilities side of a balance sheet represented the financing of the asset side. The two combined were what Minsky called a financing structure. It could be a 'hedge' financing structure, if the income derived from the assets covered financial commitments at all times; or it could be a 'speculative' financing structure, if income at times fell short of commitments, but overall covered those commitments; or it could be a 'Ponzi' financing structure if income overall would not cover commitments, so that the firm would end up with expanding liabilities relative to assets. Financial fragility was marked by 'deteriorating' financing structures, with 'hedge' financing becoming 'speculative' and 'speculative' financing becoming 'Ponzi' finance. For Minsky, business investment was always speculative, unless it was wholly financed from firms' reserves or internal finance. But investment is crucial because it generates sales revenue and in this way circulates the liquidity in balance sheets around other balance sheets in the economy. The balance sheets in the economy set a threshold which business investment must achieve to secure expected payments on debt liabilities. When investment falls below this threshold, balance sheets deteriorate as a prelude to financial crisis.

The financial instability hypothesis therefore explains how financial crisis breaks out because of inadequate business investment, rather than because of interdependent balance sheets (economic units whose assets are the liabilities of other economic units), or because of falling asset prices, as some journalists interpreters of Minsky have suggested.

In practice there are two complications that suggest inconsistencies in Minsky's analysis. The first is the issue of equity finance. This, in Minsky's view, is a classic form of 'hedge' finance, because financial commitments are contingent upon adequate operating profits. Recent economic booms in the United States and in Britain have been marked by shifts towards equity financing, and hence a more stable and sustainable form of finance. Yet, despite the equity booms of the 1980s and 1990s, financial crises broke out at the end of the 1990s and after 2008. A second complication is the existence of deposits that are the counterpart of borrowing to finance investment. These deposits must appear somewhere and would normally emerge as the profits of firms in the economy. Debt-financed investment may therefore provide its own 'hedge' (although not necessarily for the firms incurring the debt).

14.1   THE EVOLUTION OF CAPITALISM TOWARDS FINANCE

In the final years of his life, Minsky turned towards a reconsideration of the institutional foundations of his analysis, placing them in their historical context. Characteristically, he did this in the form of a reflection on the work of his doctoral supervisor, Joseph Schumpeter. In a paper entitled 'Schumpeter and Finance', Minsky explained how finance came to have the role in capitalism that he ascribed to it in his financial instability hypothesis.[1] He argued that modern capitalism had developed out of 'mercantile capitalism' (in which banks merely provide finance for trade). The greatly increased financial requirements of industrial capitalism, to finance fixed capital with a much longer period of turnover or return, gave rise to 'finance capitalism'. This was not quite the finance capitalism that Hilferding made famous in Europe. It was effectively a kind of capitalism in which investment bankers played a key role in the issue and management of long-term debt securities and stocks. In turn, this was associated with the creation of trusts and cartels to regulate the values of financial assets. 'The great crash of 1929–1933 marked the end of the era in which investment bankers dominated financial markets.'[2]

Following the 1929 Crash, capitalism evolved into what Minsky called 'managerial capitalism' in which financial pressures on firms were minimised in the interests of corporate management, with governments guaranteeing stable cash flows through the management of aggregate demand. This, in turn, bred its own downfall through the emergence of private pensions and mutual funds, resulting in 'money manager capitalism', although its predominance was not dated as precisely as the downfall of 'finance capitalism'. This reinstated the power of fund managers and, with financial innovation, the possibilities of highly leveraged speculation. In turn, in Minsky's view, such speculation led to reductions in the 'cushions of safety' (the liquidity ratios necessary to avoid forced asset sales, or forced indebtedness, to keep asset values stable). This meant that the US economy was much more vulnerable again to financial crisis: 'The question of whether a financial structure that commits a large part of cash flows to debt validation leads to a debacle such as took place between 1929 and 1933, is now an open question.'[3]

However, missing from the analysis is any distinction between different types of capitalist enterprise in the different phases through which capitalism has evolved. In one respect this may be justified. Minsky followed Kalecki and Keynes in his insistence that fixed capital investment largely determines the liquidity of capitalist firms and their ability to service their debts. The firms that invest on any significant scale are the large firms that operate in the markets for long-term debt and stocks. However, in virtually every country, there is a large segment of small and medium-sized enterprises, which provide the bulk of private sector employment. Minsky's analysis is framed as if to suggest that this sector does not exist. Moreover, small and medium-sized enterprises have relatively restricted access to debt markets, a disadvantage that has been widely discussed since the nineteenth century. The existence of such an important sector in production and employment requires a more complex analysis than the one implicit in Minsky's work where, outside the government sector, only big business operates.[4]

Hyman P. Minsky was almost unique among economists in considering how modern capitalism operates with a complex financial system at its disposal, or in charge of that capitalism, with economic instability and financial crisis imminent at all times, even in periods of apparent 'tranquillity'. For this reason he remains an authority to which economists turn in times of crisis and instability, when the inadequacies of equilibrium theories of capitalism appear most apparent. After an early start in Marshallian partial equilibrium analysis, Minsky moved on to a business cycle approach in which financial commitments and cash flows determine the expenditures of firms, in particular their investment which is the key factor in business profitability. This approach allowed Minsky to reflect in a complex way on economic and financial dynamics in a way that was almost unique among macroeconomists in the second half of the twentieth century. The inconsistencies in his vision, over money and credit, the rise of equity, and the heterogeneity of capitalist enterprise, do not detract from his importance in keeping alive the theory of credit cycles through the latter half of the twentieth century, when the real effects of credit and interest were deemed of minor significance. The revival of interest in his work after his death indicates the seriousness of the financial crises that have occurred and the lasting relevance of his analysis.

14.2 AFTER MINSKY

Minsky thought in a complex way about a complex world. The complexity of his thought and the casual jargon of the financial markets has allowed many interpreters to put forward his views or link their own views to his in a way that is often only tenuously connected with the financial macroeconomic theory of Minsky, or focusing on only one aspect or phase of his work. Interpretations of Minsky that are based on only one or a partial aspect of his theory must also be judged according to how much they tell us about his theory. In some cases, this can be very little indeed.

Interpretations have naturally proliferated since the financial crisis that broke out in the United States in 2008 and found an economics profession, which had been assured by the Nobel Laureate Robert Lucas, in his 2003 Presidential Address to the American Economics Association that the 'central problem of depression prevention has in fact been largely solved for many decades', a solution that now rendered that profession largely bereft of a language and theory with which to understand their area of expertise. Shortly after it started, Paul McCulley, an analyst with the fund manager PIMCO, referred to the fall in residential property values that was occurring as a 'Minsky Moment'. By this he meant any significant fall in asset prices that precipitates a financial crisis. The term was taken up by a leader article in the British newspaper *The Guardian* on 22 August 2007: 'Named after the economist Hyman Minsky, the phrase describes a situation where investors who have borrowed too much are forced to sell even good assets to pay back their loans ... That scenario applied right now, prompting a craze among investors for quoting the American economist.'

The fall in asset or collateral values is of course a feature of financial crisis. But in Minsky's analysis it is a symptom, rather than a cause of the crisis, and Minsky was by no means the first to identify the association of falls in asset prices with financial crisis: the association had been noted in the nineteenth century by, for example, John Stuart Mill. Nevertheless, the dubbing of the turning point in financial speculation as the 'Minsky Moment' is perhaps a worthy tribute to the only significant economist of the late twentieth century who was able to think about finance outside the framework of general equilibrium in which all problems disappear or are rendered trivial.

Among more informed commentators, the element that most interpreters have most commonly drawn from Minsky's theory is his taxonomy of financing structures, that is, his notion that balance sheets are 'hedged' 'speculative' or 'Ponzi' according to whether the income from assets covers the payment commitments of liabilities at any one time. Financial fragility therefore consists of the 'deterioration' of these financing structures from 'hedged' to speculative, and from speculative to 'Ponzi' financing. Minsky had a very specific explanation of how this deterioration came about (see below), although in his final years he referred to this process in rather more general terms.

But the taxonomy itself serves as a less than comprehensive, possibly even poor, descriptor of Minsky's theory. There are many situations that may give rise to the incidence of such structures, just as a 'Minsky Moment' may be precipitated by factors unrelated to Minsky's theory, e.g. war, taxation, and so on. For example, it is well known that illiquidity in the financial markets can cause 'forced' selling of assets and a decline in asset and collateral values, so that financing structures 'deteriorate'. Minsky observed in his *Stabilizing an Unstable Economy* that a 'Credit Crunch' in 1966 precipitated action by the Federal Reserve to make liquidity available to the markets and stabilise them. As Minsky noted 'A money-market panic, however, is ephemeral, the result of real liquidity stringency and a rapidly increasing precautionary demand funds designed to protect against awesome, unknown contingencies. As was true for some of the money-market panics of the nineteenth century, the air of crisis evaporated when the authorities finally took some action.'[5] Both Martin Wolfson and Randall Wray have pointed out that the 'crisis' was indeed a temporary illiquidity, rather than a proper Minsky crisis. As Minsky had noted, a subsequent fall in business investment in the United States was offset by a rapidly growing fiscal deficit.[6]

A second possible cause of deteriorating financing structures is policy error. Here the policy of the central bank is crucial, with Minsky himself arguing that tight money and higher interest rates cause deterioration in financing structures and crisis, such as in the case of the Penn Central Railroad failure in 1970.[7] Many of the followers of Minsky have taken up this theme to argue that it is financial liberalisation and deregulation that has 'caused' deteriorating financing structures.[8] Bad debts may of course arise as a result of bad government policy or regulation. But even if he regarded 'Big Government' as part of the solution to the problem of financial fragility, this was not a problem created by government. In fact, and at least from the 1980s, Minsky was concerned to show that crisis is in fact endogenous to a capitalist system with a complex financial system and therefore does not depend on policy 'shocks' or errors. As Minsky put it succinctly: 'capitalism is unstable because it is a financial and accumulating system'.[9] It may be noted that Minsky's remarks on securitisation highlight only upon the effect of this financial innovation on the liquidity of banks assets and hence in making money even more endogenous (rather than exogenous as monetarists believed, at the time of Minsky's remarks). However, the notes that accompany Minsky's remarks in their published version as a Levy Institute Working Paper suggest that policy encouraging this innovation gave rise directly to the sub-prime mortgage crisis, in which securitisation played such a notorious part.[10]

Since the financial crisis of 2008, perhaps the most common interpretation of Minsky's theory is the view that financial risk is exogenous and may be known to individual 'agents'. Policy to stabilise the financial system therefore makes 'agents', banks in particular, behave in a more risky way, expanding their borrowing, moving out on some Markowitz risk-return frontier, and eventually bringing on a debt crisis. 'Stability is ... destabilising'[11] because 'agents' reduce their stocks of liquid assets, or 'cushions of safety' in the belief that the government, or financial authorities will provide liquidity and lower interest rates to prevent any crisis.[12] Such a growing expectation of reward from financial operations is commonly associated with reducing liquidity preference or risk aversion as 'agents' come to believe that taking greater risks will pay off because of the belief that the authorities will step in to prevent any actual crisis – what after 2000 came to be referred to as the 'Greenspan put', the belief that the central bank would ensure that there was no possibility of loss in financial markets. There are numerous papers presenting this as an interpretation of Minsky's view,[13] most commonly using the build-up of debts in the economy à la Fisher's debt deflation, and in line with Minsky's own presentation of his financial instability hypothesis in between publication of *John Maynard Keynes* ('The debt-base ... grows at an accelerating rate during a boom ... [and] require increasing servicing as they grow... Realized quasi-rents which ultimately in real terms can grow at only a steady rate become in these circumstances an inadequate source of the cash that debt servicing requires'[14]) and *Stabilizing an Unstable Economy*.

There are two flaws in this interpretation of Minsky. First of all this view of 'risk' in the economy, due to the build-up of debt is not 'stock-flow consistent' in that it does not explain what has happened to the credit that is the counterpart of the debt financing of investment during the economic boom. It must be held by 'agents' somewhere in the system. This may not matter very much, since there is very little evidence that Minsky, for all his concern about 'balance sheet operations' in the economy, cared for 'stock-flow consistency' as a methodological principle of economic analysis. The principle itself was more an interest of Minsky's successor at the Levy Institute, Wynne Godley. However, an essential element of Minsky's theory, in the mature version that he presented in *Stabilizing an Unstable Economy*, is the reflux theory of profits. As he put it:

> Capitalist spending on investment goods leads to profits ... [which] affect investment and determine the ability of business to validate debts ... The inherent instability of capitalism is due to the way profits depend upon investment, the validation of profits depends upon profit, and investment upon the availability of external financing.[15]

This leads to the second flaw in this interpretation of Minsky. This is that it postulates exogenous risks that are undertaken by profit-maximising 'agents' (usually banks) for the sake of maximising profits. But, as Minsky made clear, these risks are not exogenous, they are endogenous: they are incurred by firms (i.e. non-financial corporations) rather than banks, even if their consequences appear on the balance sheets of banks:

> The cash flows that validate capital assets, debt structures and business styles result from investments, government deficits, balance of trade surpluses, and consumption out of incomes that are allocations to profits ... A decline in the sum of investment, government deficit, balance-of-trade surplus, and consumption out of wages and profits, decreases the validating cash flows.[16]

It is the level of investment (and the fiscal deficit and the trade surplus) in relation to the debt structures inherited from previous periods that determines the riskiness of those debt structures. At a certain level and above, debt structures are validated. Below that level, problems arise in the economy with debt commitments. A curious feature of all the 'Minskyan' interpretations of the crisis since 2008 is the absence of any discussion of the role in that crisis that was played by the fall in business investment.

The vulgarisation (in no pejorative sense) of Minsky's ideas is an inevitable consequence of the acceptance of some of those ideas into the mainstream of economic discussion. Much the same has happened with every original theorist whose work 'found its time', as Minsky did in 2008, as Keynes did in the 1930s and, before him, Marx from the 1880s. The inconsistencies between interpretations of Minsky and the theory that inspired them, as it evolved, does not of course invalidate the insights that such interpretations may offer into the ways in which debt affects capitalist dynamics. But it makes those interpretations a poor guide to the theory and ideas of Hyman Minsky.

NOTES

1. Minsky 1992.
2. Minsky 1992, p. 109.
3. Ibid., pp. 112–113.
4. See, for example, Minsky 1986, pp. 315–318.
5. Ibid., p. 90.
6. Wray 1999; Wolfson 1999.
7. Minsky 1986, pp. 91–92.
8. E.g. Arestis 2001; Barbera and Weise 2010.
9. Minsky 1986, p. 294.
10. Minsky 2008.
11. Minsky 1975, p. 127.
12. 'Two margins of safety for a firm that finances investment externally are the liquid assets held in portfolios and the excess of the present value of the expected quasi-rents from the project over the full costs of its completion' (Minsky 1986, p. 217). See Kregel 2008.
13. E.g. Assenza et al. 2010; Kregel 2008.
14. Minsky 1975, p. 143.
15. Minsky 1986, pp. 152, 294. See also Lavoie and Seccareccia 2001.
16. Minsky 1986, p. 166.

Bibliography

Aaronovitch, S. (1946) 'Agriculture in the Colonies' *Communist Review* July, pp. 21–26.

Allen, F. and Gale, D. (2004) 'Financial Fragility, Liquidity and Asset Prices' *Journal of the European Economic Association* No. 2, pp. 1015–1048.

Anderson, W.H. Locke (1964) *Corporate Finance and Fixed Investment: An Econometric Study* Cambridge, MA: Harvard University Press.

Arestis, P. (2001) 'Recent Banking and Financial Crises: Minsky versus the Financial Liberalizationists' in R. Bellofiore and P. Ferri (eds.) *Financial Keynesianism and Market Instability: The Economic Legacy of Hyman Minsky Volume 1* Cheltenham, UK and Northampton, MA, USA: Edward Elgar Publishing.

Asimakopoulos, A. (1983) 'Kalecki and Keynes on Finance, Investment and Saving' *Cambridge Journal of Economics* Vol. 7, No. 4, pp. 221–234.

Assenza, T., Delli Gatti, D. and Gallagati, M. (2010) 'Financial Instability and Agents' Heterogeneity: A Post Minskyan Research Agenda' in D.B. Papadimitriou and L.R. Wray (eds.) *The Elgar Companion to Hyman Minsky* Cheltenham, UK and Northampton, MA, USA: Edward Elgar Publishing.

Barbera, R.J. and Weise, W.L. (2010) 'It's the Right Moment to Embrace the Minsky Model' in D.B. Papadimitriou and L.R. Wray (eds.) *The Elgar Companion to Hyman Minsky* Cheltenham, UK and Northampton, MA, USA: Edward Elgar Publishing.

Bellofiore, R. (1989) 'A Monetary Labor Theory of Value' *Review of Radical Political Economics* Vol. 21, No. 1–2, pp. 1–25.

Bellofiore, R. (1998) *Essays on Volume III of Capital: Method, Value and Money* London: Macmillan.

Bellofiore, R. (2015) *German Monetary Theory Revisited* London: Palgrave Macmillan.

Bernanke, B. and Gertler, M. (1989) 'Agency Costs, Net Worth, and Business Fluctuations' *American Economic Review* Vol. 79, No. 1, pp. 14–31.

Bikhchandani, S., Hirshleifer, D. and Welch, I. (1992) 'A Theory of Fads, Fashion, Custom and Cultural Change as Information Cascades' *Journal of Political Economy* Vol. 100, No. 5, pp. 995–1026.

Bordo, M.D. (1986) 'Financial Crises, Banking Crises, Stock Market Crashes and the Money Supply: Some International Evidence, 1870–1933' in F. Capie and G.E. Wood (eds.) *Financial Crises and the World Banking System* London: Macmillan.

Breit, M. (1933) *Stopa procentowa w Polsce* Kraków: Polska Akademia Umiejętności.

Breit, M. (1935a) 'Ein Beitrag zur Theorie der Geld- und Kapitalmarktes' *Zeitschrift für Nationalökonomie* Band VI, Heft 5.

Breit, M. (1935b) 'Konjunkturalny rozwój kredytu długoterminowego w Polsce' (The Cyclical Development of Long-Term Credit in Poland) *Prace Instytutu Badań Konjunktur Gospodarczych i Cen* No. 3–4, pp. 94–98.

Breit, M. and Lange, O. (1934) 'The Way to the Socialist Planned Economy' *History of Economics Review* No. 37, Winter 2003, pp. 41–50.

de Brunhoff, S. (1976) *Marx on Money* translated by Maurice J. Goldbloom, with a Preface by Duncan K. Foley, New York: Urizen Books.

de Brunhoff, S. (1978) *The State, Capital and Economic Policy* translated by Mike Sonenscher, London: Pluto Press.

Bukharin, N.I. (1924) *Imperialism and the Accumulation of Capital*, published together with Rosa Luxemburg *The Accumulation of Capital – An Anti-Critique* translated by Rudolf Wichman, and edited and translated by Kenneth J. Tarbuck, New York and London: Monthly Review Press 1972.

Capie, F., Mills, T.C. and Wood, G.E. (1986) 'What Happened in 1931?' in F. Capie and G.E. Wood (eds.) *Financial Crises and the World Banking System* London: Macmillan.

Chick, V. (1983) *Macroeconomics After Keynes: A Reconsideration of the General Theory* Cambridge, MA: MIT Press.

Chick, V. (1986) 'The Evolution of the Banking System and the Theory of Saving, Investment and Interest' in S.C. Dow and P. Arestis (eds.) *On Money, Method and Keynes: Selected Essays* London: Macmillan 1992.

Chick, V. (1987) 'Hugh Townshend' in J. Eatwell, M. Milgate and P. Newman (eds.) *The New Palgrave: A Dictionary of Economics* London: Macmillan.

Chick, V. (1993) 'Sources of Finance, Recent Changes in Bank Behaviour and the Theory of Investment and Interest' in P. Arestis (ed.) *Money and Banking: Issues for the 21st Century* London: Macmillan.

Chick, V. (1996) 'Equilibrium and Determination in Open Systems: The Case of the General Theory' *History of Economics Review* No. 25, Winter–Summer, pp. 184–188.

Chilosi, A. (1982) 'Breit, Kalecki and Hicks on the Term Structure of Interest Rates, Risk and the Theory of Investment' in M. Baranzini (ed.) *Advances in Economic Theory* Oxford: Basil Blackwell.

Clarke, S. (1994) *Marx's Theory of Crisis* Basingstoke: Macmillan.

Committee on Finance and Industry (The Macmillan Committee) (1931) *Report* London: HMSO.

Corry, B. (1962) *Money, Saving, and Investment in English Economics, 1800–1850* London: Macmillan.

Davidson, P. (1978) *Money and the Real World* London: Macmillan.

Deutscher, P. (1990) *R.G. Hawtrey and the Development of Macroeconomics* London: Macmillan.

Dimand, R.W. (2000) 'Irving Fisher and the Quantity Theory of Money: The Last Phase' *Journal of the History of Economic Thought* Vol. 22, No. 3, pp. 329–348.

Dow, J.C.R. and Saville, I.D. (1988) *A Critique of Monetary Policy: Theory and British Experience* Oxford: Clarendon Press.

Ellis, H.S. (1934) *German Monetary Theory 1905–1933* Cambridge, MA: Harvard University Press.

Emery, H.C. (1896) *Speculation on the Stock and Produce Exchanges of the United States* New York: Columbia University Press, reprinted New York: AMS Press 1968.

Engels, F. (1970a) 'Preface' in K. Marx, *Capital: A Critique of Political Economy Volume III: The Process of Capitalist Production as a Whole* London: Lawrence & Wishart.

Engels, F. (1970b) 'Supplement to *Capital* Volume Three' in K. Marx, *Capital: A Critique of Political Economy Volume III: The Process of Capitalist Production as a Whole* London: Lawrence & Wishart.

Eshag, E. (1963) *From Marshall to Keynes* Oxford: Basil Blackwell.

Fisher, I. (1907) *The Rate of Interest: Its Nature, Determination and Relation to Economic Phenomena* New York: Macmillan.

Fisher, I. (1911) *The Purchasing Power of Money: Its Determination and Relation to Credit, Interest and Crises* New York: Macmillan.

Fisher, I. (1930) *The Stock Market Crash – And After* New York: Macmillan.

Fisher, I. (1932) *Booms and Depressions* New York: Adelphi Company.

Fisher, I. (1933) 'The Debt Deflation Theory of Great Depressions' *Econometrica* Vol. 1, No. 1, pp. 337–357.

Fisher, I. (1936) 'The Depression: Its Causes and Cures' in C.H. Sisam (ed.) *Abstracts of Papers Presented at the Research Conference on Economics and Statistics Held by the Cowles Commission for Research in Economics at Colorado College, July 6 to August 8 1936* Colorado Springs, CO: Colorado College Publication, General Series, No. 208, pp. 104–107.

Friedman, M. (1967) 'The Monetary Theory and Policy of Henry Simons' The Third Henry Simons Lecture delivered at the Law School, University of Chicago, 5 May 1967, reprinted in *The Optimum Quantity of Money and Other Essays*, Hawthorne, NY: Aldine Publishing Company 1969.

Friedman, M. (1968) 'The Role of Monetary Policy' *American Economic Review* Vol. 58, No. 1, pp. 1–17.

Friedman, M. (1986) 'The Resource Costs of Irredeemable Paper Money' *Journal of Political Economy* Vol. 4, pp. 642–647.

Friedman, M. and Schwartz, A.J. (1963) *A Monetary History of the United States 1867–1960* Princeton, NJ: Princeton University Press for the National Bureau of Economic Research.

Galbraith, J.K. (1980) *The Great Crash* London: André Deutsch.

Gilbert, J.C. (1982) *Keynes's Impact on Monetary Economics* London: Butterworth & Co.

Goodhart, C.A.E. (1987) 'Why do Banks Need a Central Bank?' *Oxford Economic Papers* Vol. 39.

Goodhart, C.A.E. (1988) *The Evolution of Central Banks* Cambridge, MA: MIT Press.

Goodhart, C.A.E. (2001) 'What Weight Should Be Given to Asset Prices in the Measurement of Inflation?' *Economic Journal* Vol. 111, No. 472, pp. F335–F356.

Gootzeit, M.J. (1999) 'Marshall's vs Wicksell's Theory of the Cumulative Process' *History of Economics Review* No. 29, Winter, pp. 16–30.

Halevi, J. and Taouil, R. (2002) 'On a Post-Keynesian Stream from France and Italy: The Circuit Approach' in P. Arestis, M. Desai and S.C. Dow (eds.) *Money, Macroeconomics and Keynes: Essays in Honour of Victoria Chick* London: Routledge.

Hansen, A.H. (1927) *Business Cycle Theory: Its Development and Present Status* Boston, MA: Athenaeum.

Hansen, A.H. (1953) *A Guide to Keynes* New York: McGraw-Hill.

Harcourt, G.C. and O'Shaughnessy, T.J. (1985) 'Keynes's Unemployment Equilibrium: Some Insights from Joan Robinson, Piero Sraffa and Richard Kahn' in G.C. Harcourt (ed.) *Keynes and His Contemporaries* London: Macmillan.

Harrod, R.F. (1936) *The Trade Cycle: An Essay* Oxford: Clarendon Press.

Harrod, R.F. (1951) *The Life of John Maynard Keynes* London: Macmillan.

Hawtrey, R.G. (1913) *Good and Bad Trade: An Inquiry into the Causes of Trade Fluctuations* London: Constable, republished with a new Foreword by the author, New York: Augustus M. Kelley 1962.

Hawtrey, R.G. (1925) 'Public Expenditure and the Demand for Labour' *Economica* Vol. 5, March, pp. 38–48.

Hawtrey, R.G. (1931) *Trade Depression and the Way Out* London: Longmans, Green and Co.

Hawtrey, R.G. (1933) *The Art of Central Banking* London: Longmans, Green and Co.

Hawtrey, R.G. (1934) *Currency and Credit* (third edition) London: Longmans, Green and Co.

Hawtrey, R.G. (1937) *Capital and Employment* London: Longmans, Green and Co.

Hawtrey, R.G. (1938) *A Century of Bank Rate* London: Longmans, Green and Co.

Hawtrey, R.G. (1961) 'Foreword' to 1962 edition of Hawtrey (1913).

Hawtrey, R.G. (1962) *A Century of Bank Rate* London: Frank Cass.

Hayek, F.A. (1932) 'Note on the Development of the Doctrine of Forced Saving' *Quarterly Journal of Economics* Vol. 47, pp. 123–133.

Hayek, F.A. (1935) *Prices and Production* New York: Augustus M. Kelly 1967.

Hayek, F.A. (1946) 'The Meaning of Competition' in *Individualism and Economic Order* London: Routledge & Kegan Paul 1949.

Hayek, F.A. (1976) *The Denationalization of Money* London: Institute of Economic Affairs.

Hein, E. (2012) *The Macroeconomics of Finance-Dominated Capitalism – And Its Crisis* Cheltenham, UK and Northampton, MA, USA: Edward Elgar Publishing.

Hicks, J. (1933) 'Gleichgewicht und Konjunktur' *Zeitschrift für Nationalökonomie* Band IV, Heft IV; revised English version 'Equilibrium and the Cycle' in *Money, Interest and Wages, Collected Essays on Economic Theory* Oxford: Basil Blackwell 1982.

Hicks, J. (1935) 'A Suggestion for Simplifying the Theory of Money' *Economica* New series No. 2, pp. 1–19, reprinted in *Critical Essays in Monetary Theory* Oxford: Clarendon Press 1967.

Hicks, J. (1977) *Economic Perspectives* Oxford: Clarendon Press.

Hilferding, R. (1910) *Finance Capital: A Study of the Latest Phase of Capitalist Development* edited and introduced by Tom Bottomore, translated by Morris Watnick and Sam Gordon, London: Routledge & Kegan Paul 1981.

Hobson, J.A. (1913) *Gold, Prices and Wages with an Examination of the Quantity Theory* London: Methuen.

Hobson, J.A. (1938a) *Imperialism: A Study* London: George Allen & Unwin.

Hobson, J.A. (1938b) *Confessions of an Economic Heretic* London: George Allen & Unwin.

Howard, M. (1983) *Profits in Economic Theory* London: Macmillan.

Howson, S. (1975) *Domestic Money Management in Britain 1919–1938* Cambridge: Cambridge University Press.

Howson, S. (1985) 'Hawtrey and the Real World' in G.C. Harcourt (ed.) *Keynes and His Contemporaries* London: Macmillan.

Howson, S. and Winch, D. (1977) *The Economic Advisory Council 1930–1939: A Study in Economic Advice during Depression and Recovery* Cambridge: Cambridge University Press.

Kahn, R.F. (1972) 'Notes on Liquidity Preference' in *Selected Essays on Employment and Growth* Cambridge: Cambridge University Press.

Kaldor, N. (1938) 'Hawtrey on Short- and Long-Term Investment' *Economica* November, republished in *Essays on Economic Stability and Growth* London: Gerald Duckworth & Co. 1960.

Kaldor, N. (1939) 'Speculation and Economic Stability' republished in *Essays on Economic Stability and Growth* London: Gerald Duckworth & Co. 1960.

Kaldor, N. (1960) 'Introduction' to *Essays on Economic Stability and Growth* London: Gerald Duckworth & Co.

Kaldor, N. (1982) *The Scourge of Monetarism* Oxford: Oxford University Press.

Kalecki, M. (1932) 'Inflacja a Wojna' *Przegląd Socjalistyczny* Vol. 2, No. 13, pp. 1–2.

Kalecki, M. (1932) 'Inflation and War' in J. Osiatynski (ed.) *Collected Works of Michal Kalecki Volume VI: Studies in Applied Economics 1927–1941* Oxford: Clarendon Press 1996.

Kalecki, M. (1933a) 'Stimulating the World Business Upswing' translated by Chester Adam Kisiel in J. Osiatyński (ed.) *Collected Works of Michał Kalecki Volume I: Capitalism: Business Cycles and Full Employment* Oxford: Clarendon Press 1990.

Kalecki, M. (1933b) 'O handlu zagranicznym I "eksporcie wewnętrznym"' *Ekonomista* No. 3, pp. 27–35.

Kalecki, M. (1933/1990) 'Outline of the Business Cycle Theory' in J. Osiatyński (ed.) *Collected Works of Michał Kalecki Volume I: Capitalism: Business Cycles and Full Employment* Oxford: Clarendon Press 1990.

Kalecki, M. (1936–1937) 'A Theory of the Business Cycle' *Review of Economic Studies* Vol. 4, No. 2, pp. 77–97.

Kalecki, M. (1937) 'The Principle of Increasing Risk' *Economica* Vol. 4, No. 16, pp. 440–446.

Kalecki, M. (1938) 'Review of *Die Aufgaben des Geldes*' *Economic Journal* Vol. 48 No. 1, pp. 76–77.

Kalecki, M. (1939) *Essays in the Theory of Economic Fluctuations* London: George Allen & Unwin.

Kalecki, M. (1940) 'The Short-Term Rate and the Long-Term Rate' *Oxford Economic Papers* No. 4, September, pp. 15–22.

Kalecki, M. (1943) *Studies in Economic Dynamics* London: George Allen & Unwin.

Kalecki, M. (1944) 'Professor Pigou on "The Classic Stationary State": A Comment' *Economic Journal* Vol. 54, No. 1, pp. 131–132.

Kalecki, M. (1945) 'The Maintenance of Full Employment after the Transition Period: A Comparison of the Problem in the USA and the UK' *International Labour Review* Vol. 52, No. 5, pp. 449–464.

Kalecki, M. (1950) 'A New Approach to Problem of Business Cycles' *Review of Economic Studies* Vol. 17, No. 2, pp. 57–64.

Kalecki, M. (1954) *Theory of Economic Dynamics: An Essay on Cyclical and Long-Run Changes in Capitalist Economy* London: George Allen & Unwin.

Kalecki, M. (1968a) 'Trend and the Business Cycle' in *Selected Essays on the Dynamics of the Capitalist Economy 1933–1970* Cambridge: Cambridge University Press 1971.

Kalecki, M. (1968b) 'Trend and Business Cycles Reconsidered' *Economic Journal* Vol. 78, No. 2, pp. 263–276.

Keynes, J.M. (1911) 'Review of Irving Fisher The Purchasing Power of Money: Its Determination and Relation to Credit, Interest and Crises' *Economic Journal* September, reprinted in D. Moggridge (ed.) *The Collected Writings of John Maynard Keynes Volume XI: Economic Articles and Correspondence Academic* London: Macmillan, Cambridge University Press for the Royal Economic Society 1973.

Keynes, J.M. (1912) 'Review of W. Stanley Jevons Theory of Political Economy' *Economic Journal* March, reprinted in D. Moggridge (ed.) *The Collected Writings of John Maynard Keynes Volume XI: Economic Articles and Correspondence Academic* London: Macmillan, Cambridge University Press for the Royal Economic Society 1973.

Keynes, J.M. (1913) 'How Far are Bankers Responsible for Alternations of Crisis and Depression?' reprinted in D. Moggridge (ed.) *The Collected Writings of John Maynard Keynes Volume XIII: The General Theory and After Part 1: Preparation* London: Macmillan for the Royal Economic Society 1973.

Keynes, J.M. (1915) 'Review of Mrs. Russell Barrington (ed.) The Works and Life of Walter Bagehot' *Economic Journal* September, reprinted in D. Moggridge (ed.) *The Collected Writings of John Maynard Keynes Volume XI: Economic Articles and Correspondence Academic* London: Macmillan, Cambridge University Press for the Royal Economic Society 1973.

Keynes, J.M. (1930) *A Treatise on Money in Two Volumes. 1: The Pure Theory of Money. 2: The Applied Theory of Money* London: Macmillan & Co.

Keynes, J.M. (1931a) 'Credit Control' *The Encyclopaedia of the Social Sciences* reprinted in D. Moggridge (ed.) *The Collected Writings of John Maynard Keynes Volume XI: Economic Articles and Correspondence Academic* London: Macmillan, Cambridge University Press for the Royal Economic Society 1973.

Keynes, J.M. (1931b) 'An Economic Analysis of Unemployment' The Harris Lectures reprinted in D. Moggridge (ed.) *The Collected Writings of John Maynard Keynes Volume XIII: The General Theory and After Part 1: Preparation* London: Macmillan for the Royal Economic Society 1973.

Keynes, J.M. (1933a) 'Mr. Keynes's Control Scheme' *American Economic Review* December, reprinted in D. Moggridge (ed.) *The Collected Writings of John Maynard Keynes Volume XI: Economic Articles and Correspondence Academic* London: Macmillan, Cambridge University Press for the Royal Economic Society 1973.

Keynes, J.M. (1933b) 'A Monetary Theory of Production' reprinted in D. Moggridge (ed.) *The Collected Writings of John Maynard Keynes Volume XIII: The General Theory and After Part 1: Preparation* London: Macmillan for the Royal Economic Society 1973.

Keynes, J.M. (1935) 'Comments on D.H.R.'s Criticisms' reprinted in D. Moggridge (ed.) *The Collected Writings of John Maynard Keynes Volume XIII: The General Theory and After Part 1: Preparation* London: Macmillan for the Royal Economic Society 1973.

Keynes, J.M. (1936) *The General Theory of Employment, Interest and Money* London: Macmillan & Co.

Keynes, J.M. (1937a) 'The General Theory of Employment' *Quarterly Journal of Economics* Vol. 51, No. 2 reprinted in D. Moggridge (ed.) *The Collected Writings of John Maynard Keynes Volume XIV: The General Theory and After Part 2: Defence and Development* London: Macmillan for the Royal Economic Society 1973.

Keynes, J.M. (1937b) 'Alternative Theories of the Rate of Interest' *Economic Journal* Vol. 47, June, reprinted in D. Moggridge (ed.) *The Collected Writings of John Maynard Keynes Volume XIV: The General Theory and After Part 2: Defence and Development* London: Macmillan for the Royal Economic Society 1973.

Keynes, J.M. (1937c) 'The Ex-Ante Theory of the Rate of Interest' *Economic Journal* Vol. 47, December, pp. 663–669.

Keynes, J.M. (1945) 'The National Debt Enquiry: Lord Keynes's Notes' reprinted in D. Moggridge (ed.) *The Collected Writings of John Maynard Keynes Volume XXVII: Activities 1940–1946 Shaping the Post-War World: Employment and Commodities* London: Macmillan, Cambridge University Press for the Royal Economic Society 1980.

Keynes, J.M. (1973a) *The Collected Writings of John Maynard Keynes Volume XIII: The General Theory and After, Part 1: Preparation* edited by Donald Moggridge, London: Macmillan for the Royal Economic Society.

Keynes, J.M. (1973b) *The Collected Writings of John Maynard Keynes Volume XIV: The General Theory and After, Part 2: Defence and Development* edited by Donald Moggridge, London: Macmillan for the Royal Economic Society.

Keynes, J.M. (1979) *The Collected Writings of John Maynard Keynes Volume XXIX: The General Theory and After, A Supplement* edited by Donald Moggridge, London: Macmillan, Cambridge University Press for the Royal Economic Society.

Keynes, J.M. (1983) *The Collected Writings of John Maynard Keynes Volume XII: Economic Articles and Correspondence: Investment and Editorial* London: Macmillan for the Royal Economic Society.

Kindleberger, C.P. (1993) *A Financial History of Western Europe* Oxford: Oxford University Press.

Klein, L.R. (1947) *The Keynesian Revolution* New York: Macmillan.

Kowalik, T. (1992) *Historia Ekonomii w Polsce 1864–1950* Wrocław: Zakład Narodowy im. Ossolińskich.

Kowalik, T. (2014) *Rosa Luxemburg: Theory of Accumulation and Imperialism* Basingstoke: Palgrave Macmillan.

Kregel, J. (1989) 'Savings, Investment and Finance in Kalecki's Theory' in M. Sebastiani (ed.) *Kalecki's Relevance Today* London: Macmillan.

Kregel, J. (2008) 'Changes in the U.S. Financial System and the Sub-Prime Crisis' *Working Paper* No. 50, Annandale-on-Hudson, NY: Jerome Levy Economics Institute of Bard College.

Laidler, D. (1991) *The Golden Age of the Quantity Theory* Princeton, NJ: Princeton University Press.

Laidler, D. (1999) *Fabricating the Keynesian Revolution: Studies of the Inter-War Literature on Money, the Cycle and Unemployment* Cambridge: Cambridge University Press.

Lavington, F. (1921) *The English Capital Market* London: Methuen, reprinted New York: Augustus M. Kelley 1968.

Lavoie, M. and Seccareccia, M. (2001) 'Minsky's Financial Fragility Hypothesis: A Missing Macroeconomic Link?' in R. Bellofiore and P. Ferri (eds.) *Financial Fragility and Investment in the Capitalist Economy: The Economic Legacy of Hyman Minsky Volume II* Cheltenham, UK and Northampton, MA, USA: Edward Elgar Publishing.

Lawlor, M.S. (1994) 'On the Historical Origin of Keynes's Financial Market Views' in N. De Marchi and Mary S. Morgan (eds.) *Higgling, Transactors and Their Markets in the History of Economics* Annual Supplement to volume 26 *History of Political Economy* Durham, NC and London: Duke University Press.

Lenin, V.I. (1917) 'Imperialism, the Highest Stage of Capitalism' in *Selected Works* Moscow: Progress Publishers 1968.

Lucas, R.E. (1981) *Studies in Business Cycle Theory* Oxford: Basil Blackwell.

Luxemburg, R. (1951) *The Accumulation of Capital* translated by Agnes Schwartzschild, London: Routledge & Kegan Paul.

MacLachlan, F.C. (1993) *Keynes's General Theory of Interest: A Reconsideration* London: Routledge.

Marshall, A. (1899) 'The Folly of Amateur Speculators Makes the Fortunes of Professionals: The Wiles of Some Professionals' in M. Dardi and M. Gallegati 'Marshall on Speculation' *History of Political Economy* Vol. 24, No. 3, 1992, pp. 571–593.

Marshall, A. (1924) *Money, Credit and Commerce* London: Macmillan.
Marshall, A. (1938) *Principles of Economics* London: Macmillan.
Marshall, A. and Marshall, M.P. (1879) *The Economics of Industry* Bristol: Thoemmes Press 1994.
Marx, K. (1932) *Das Kapital, Kritik der Politischen Ökonomie, Dritter Bank, Buch III, Der Gesamtprozess der kapitalistischen Produktion* Berlin: Dietz Verlag.
Marx, K. (1959) *Capital: A Critique of Political Economy Volume III: The Process of Capitalist Production as a Whole* edited by F. Engels, Moscow: Progress Publishers.
Marx, K. (1974) *Capital: A Critique of Political Economy Volume II: The Process of Circulation of Capital* edited by F. Engels, London: Lawrence & Wishart.
Marx, K. (1975) *Theories of Surplus Value, Volume IV of Capital, Part III* Moscow: Progress Publishers.
Marx, K. (1993) *Grundrisse: Foundations of the Critique of Political Economy (Rough Draft)* London: Penguin Books.
Marx, K. and Engels, F. (1936) *Selected Correspondence 1846–1895* translated with Commentary and Notes by Dona Torr, London: Lawrence & Wishart.
Marx, K. and Engels, F. (1992) *Collected Works Volume 46: Marx and Engels 1880–1883* London: Lawrence & Wishart.
Meulen, H. (1934) *Free Banking: An Outline of a Policy of Individualism* London: Macmillan.
Michell, J. and Toporowski, J. (2013–2014) 'Critical Observations on Financialization and Financial Process' *International Journal of Political Economy* Vol. 42, No. 4, pp. 67–82.
Mill, J.S. (1826) 'Paper Currency – Commercial Distress' *The Parliamentary History and Review* Vol. II, cited in Corry 1962, pp. 104–105.
Minsky, H.P. (1954/2004) *Induced Investment and Business Cycles* edited and with an Introduction by Dimitri B. Papadimitriou, Cheltenham, UK and Northampton, MA, USA: Edward Elgar Publishing.
Minsky, H.P. (1964) 'Financial Crisis, Financial Systems, and the Performance of the Economy' in Commission on Money and Credit (ed.), *Private Capital Markets* Englewood Cliffs, NJ: Prentice Hall.
Minsky, H.P. (1975) *John Maynard Keynes* New York: Columbia University Press.
Minsky, H.P. (1978) 'The Financial Instability Hypothesis: A Restatement' *Thames Papers in Political Economy*, London: Thames Polytechnic.
Minsky, H.P. (1982a) 'The Financial Instability Hypothesis: Capitalist Processes and the Behaviour of the Economy' in C.P. Kindleberger and J.-P. Laffargue (eds.) *Financial Crisis: Theory, History, Policy* Cambridge: Cambridge University Press.
Minsky, H.P. (1982b) *Inflation, Recession and Economic Policy* Brighton: Wheatsheaf Books.
Minsky, H.P. (1986) *Stabilizing an Unstable Economy* New Haven, CT: Yale University Press.
Minsky, H. P. (1988) 'Beginnings' in J.A. Kregel (ed.) *Recollections of Eminent Economists* Vol. I, Basingstoke: Macmillan.

Minsky, H.P. (1992) 'Schumpeter and Finance' in S. Biasco, A. Roncaglia and M. Salvati (eds.) *Market and Institutions in Economic Development: Essays in Honour of Paulo Sylos-Labini* London: Macmillan.

Minsky, H.P. (2008) 'Securitization' *Policy Note* No. 2, Annandale-on-Hudson, NY: Jerome Levy Economics Institute of Bard College.

Moseley, F. (ed.) (2005) *Marx's Theory of Money* Basingstoke: Palgrave Macmillan.

Mott, T. (1982) 'Kalecki's Principle of Increasing Risk: The Role of Finance in the Post-Keynesian Theory of Investment Fluctuations' PhD dissertation, Stanford University.

Mott, T. (1985–1986) 'Kalecki's Principle of Increasing Risk and the Relation Among Mark-Up Pricing, Investment Fluctuations, and Liquidity Preference' *Economic Forum* Vol. 15, Winter, pp. 65–76.

Myrdal, G. (1939) *Monetary Equilibrium* London: William Hodge and Co.

Neisser, H. (1928) *Der Tauschwert des Geldes* Jena: G. Fischer Verlag.

Nelson, A. (1998) *Marx's Concept of Money: The God of Commodities* London: Routledge.

Niebyl, K.H. (1946) *Studies in the Classical Theories of Money* New York: Columbia University Press.

Ohlin, B. (1937) 'Some Notes on the Stockholm Theory of Savings and Investment' *Economic Journal* Vol. 47, Part I, March, pp. 53–69; Part II, June, pp. 221–240.

Ohlin, B. (1965) 'Introduction' in K. Wicksell, *Interest and Prices (Geldzins und Guterpreise): A Study of the Causes Regulating the Value of Money* translated by R.F. Kahn, New York: Augustus M. Kelley.

Osiatyński, J. (ed.) (1990) *The Collected Works of Michał Kalecki Volume I: Capitalism: Business Cycles and Full Employment* Oxford: Clarendon Press.

Osiatyński, J. (ed.) (1991) *The Collected Works of Michał Kalecki Volume II: Capitalism: Economic Dynamics* Oxford: Clarendon Press.

Patinkin, D. (1961) 'The Chicago Tradition' in *Studies in Monetary Economics* New York: Harper & Row 1972.

Patinkin, D. (1982) *Anticipations of the General Theory? And Other Essays on Keynes* Oxford: Basil Blackwell.

Phillips, R.J. (1995) *The Chicago Plan & New Deal Banking Reform* Armonk, NY: M.E. Sharpe.

Polanyi, K. (1945) *The Great Transformation: The Political and Economic Origins of Our Time* London: Victor Gollancz.

Realfonzo, R. (1998) *Money and Banking: Theory and Debate (1900–1940)* Cheltenham, UK and Lyme, NH, USA: Edward Elgar Publishing.

Robertson, D.H. (1928) *Money* London: Nisbet & Co.

Robertson, D.H. (1936) 'Some Notes on Mr. Keynes's *General Theory of Employment*' *Quarterly Journal of Economics* November, p. 174.

Robertson, D.H. (1949) 'What Has Happened to the Rate of Interest?' *Three Banks Review*, March, reprinted in *Essays in Money and Interest* Selected with a Memoir by John Hicks, London: Collins/Fontana Library 1966.

Robertson, D.H. (1954) 'Thoughts on Meeting Some Important Persons' *Quarterly Journal of Economics* May, pp. 181–190.

Robinson, J.V. (1952) *The Rate of Interest and Other Essays* London: Macmillan & Co.

Robinson, J.V. (1956) *The Accumulation of Capital* London: Macmillan & Co.

Robinson, J.V. (1969) 'Introduction' to M. Kalecki *Studies in the Theory of Business Cycles 1933–1939* Oxford: Basil Blackwell.

Roll, E. (1960) *A History of Economic Thought* London: Faber and Faber.

Sawyer, M.C. (1985) *The Economics of Michał Kalecki* London: Macmillan.

Sawyer, M.C. (2001) 'Kalecki on Money and Finance' *European Journal of History of Economic Thought* Vol. 8, No. 4, pp. 487–508.

Schumpeter, J.A. (1927) 'The Explanation of the Business Cycle' *Economica* Vol. 7, pp. 286–311.

Schumpeter, J.A. (1934) *The Theory of Economic Development: An Inquiry into Profits, Capital, Credit, Interest and the Business Cycle* translated by Redvers Opie, New York: Oxford University Press 1961.

Schumpeter, J.A. (1939) *Business Cycles Volume I: A Theoretical, Historical, and Statistical Analysis of the Capitalist Process* New York: McGraw-Hill.

Schumpeter, J.A. (1954) *History of Economic Analysis* Oxford: Oxford University Press, reprinted London: Allen & Unwin 1982.

Shackle, G.L.S. (1949) 'The Nature of Interest Rates' *Oxford Economic Papers* new series, Vol. I, pp. 99–120, reprinted in *Uncertainty in Economics and Other Reflections* Cambridge: Cambridge University Press 1955.

Shackle, G.L.S. (1967) *The Years of High Theory: Invention and Tradition in Economic Thought 1926–1939* Cambridge: Cambridge University Press.

Simons, H.C. (1936) 'Rules versus Authorities in Monetary Policy' in *Economic Policy for a Free Society* Chicago: University of Chicago Press 1948.

Simons, H.C. (1942) 'Hanson on Fiscal Policy' in *Economic Policy for a Free Society* Chicago: University of Chicago Press 1948.

Simons, H.C. (1944) 'Economic Stability and Antitrust Policy' in *Economic Policy for a Free Society* Chicago: University of Chicago Press 1948.

Steindl, J. (1941) 'On Risk' *Oxford Economic Papers* No. 5, June, pp. 43–53.

Steindl, J. (1945a) 'Capitalist Enterprise and Risk' *Oxford Economic Papers* No. 7, March, pp. 21–45.

Steindl, J. (1945b) *Small and Big Business: Economic Problems of the Size of Firms* Institute of Statistics Monograph No. 1, Oxford: Basil Blackwell.

Steindl, J. (1952) *Maturity and Stagnation in American Capitalism* Institute of Statistics Monograph No. 4, Oxford: Basil Blackwell.

Steindl, J. (1965) *Random Processes and the Growth of Firms: A Study of the Pareto Law* London: Charles Griffin & Co.

Steindl, J. (1981) 'Some Comments on the Three Versions of Kalecki's Theory of the Business Cycle' in N. Assorodobraj-Kula et al. (eds.) *Studies in Economic Theory and Practice: Essays in Honour of Edward Lipiński* Amsterdam: North Holland Publishing Company.

Steindl, J. (1982) 'The Role of Household Saving in the Modern Economy' *Banca Nazionale del Lavoro Quarterly Review* No. 140, March, pp. 69–88.

Steindl, J. (1989) 'Saving and Debt' in A. Barrère (ed.) *Money, Credit and Prices in Keynesian Perspective* London: Macmillan.

Steindl, J. (1990) 'The Dispersion of Expectations in Speculative Markets' in *Economic Papers 1941–88* London: Macmillan.

Stiglitz, J.E. and Weiss, A. (1981) 'Credit Rationing in Markets with Imperfect Information' *American Economic Review* Vol. 71, pp. 393–410.

Stockhammer, E. (2012) 'Financialization' in J. Michell and J. Toporowski (eds.) *Handbook of Critical Issues in Finance* Cheltenham: Edward Elgar Publishing.

Tily, G. (2007) *Keynes's* General Theory, *The Rate of Interest, and 'Keynesian' Economics: Keynes Betrayed* Basingstoke: Palgrave Macmillan.

Tobin, J. (1969) 'A General Equilibrium Approach to Monetary Theory' *Journal of Money, Credit and Banking* No. 1, February, pp. 15–29.

Tobin, J. and Brainard, W.C. (1977) 'Asset Markets and the Cost of Capital' in R. Nelson and B. Balassa (eds.) *Economic Progress, Private Values and Public Policy: Essays in Honor of William Fellner* Amsterdam: North Holland Publishing Company.

Toporowski, J. (1993a) *The Economics of Financial Markets and the 1987 Crash* Aldershot, UK and Brookfield, VT, USA: Edward Elgar Publishing.

Toporowski, J. (1993b) 'Profits in the U.K. Economy: Some Kaleckian Models' *Review of Political Economy* Vol. 5, No. 1, pp. 40–54.

Toporowski, J. (1995) 'A Refinancing Theory of Capital Markets and Their Valuation' *Social Concept* Vol. 7, No. 1, pp. 107–128.

Toporowski, J. (1999a) 'Monetary Policy in an Era of Capital Market Inflation' *Working Paper* No. 279, Annandale-on-Hudson, NY: Jerome Levy Economics Institute of Bard College.

Toporowski, J. (1999b) 'Kalecki and the Declining Rate of Profit' *Review of Political Economy* Vol. 11, No. 3, pp. 355–371.

Toporowski, J. (2000) *The End of Finance: The Theory of Capital Market Inflation, Financial Derivatives and Pension Fund Capitalism* London: Routledge.

Toporowski, J. (2002) 'Mutual Banking from Utopia to the Capital Market' *Revue d'Économie financière* No. 67, pp. 45–55.

Toporowski, J. (2005) *Theories of Financial Disturbance: An Examination of Critical Theories of Finance from Adam Smith to the Present Day* Cheltenham, UK and Northampton, MA, USA: Edward Elgar Publishing.

Toporowski, J. (2008a) 'Minsky's "Induced Investment and Business Cycles"' *Cambridge Journal of Economics* Vol. 32, No. 5, pp. 725–737.

Toporowski, J. (2008b) 'Notes on Excess Capital and Liquidity Management' *Working Paper* No. 549, Annandale-on-Hudson, NY: Jerome Levy Economics Institute of Bard College.

Toporowski, J. (2012) 'Corporate Liquidity and Financial Fragility: The Role of Investment, Debt and Interest' *Working Paper* No. 169, Department of Economics, The School of Oriental and African Studies, University of London.

Toporowski, J. (2019) 'Marx's Observations on the Classical Theory of Interest' in S. Gupta, M. Musto and B. Amini (eds.) *Karl Marx's Life, Ideas, and Influences: A Critical Examination on the Bicentenary* Basingstoke: Palgrave Macmillan.

Toporowski, J. (2020) 'Financialisation and the Periodisation of Capitalism: Appearances and Processes' *Review of Evolutionary Political Economy* Vol. 1, No. 1.

Townshend, H. (1937) 'Liquidity-Premium and the Theory of Value' *Economic Journal* Vol. 47, No. 1, pp. 157–169.

Trigg, A.B. (2006) *Marxian Reproduction Schema: Money and Aggregate Demand in a Capitalist Economy* London: Routledge.

Varga, E. (1935) *The Great Crisis and Its Political Consequences: Economics and Politics 1928–1934* London: Modern Books Ltd.

Veblen, T. (1904) *The Theory of Business Enterprise* New York: Charles Scribner's Sons.

Vercelli, A. (2001) 'Minsky, Keynes and the Structural Instability of a Sophisticated Monetary Economy' in R. Bellofiore and P. Ferri (eds.) *Financial Fragility and Investment in the Capitalist Economy: The Economic Legacy of Hyman Minsky, Volume II* Cheltenham, UK and Northampton, MA, USA: Edward Elgar Publishing.

White, L.H. (1984) *Free Banking in Britain* Cambridge: Cambridge University Press.

Wicksell, K. (1898) *Interest and Prices* English translation, London: Macmillan 1936.

Wicksell, K. (1935) *Lectures on Political Economy Volume II: Money* translated from the Swedish by E. Classen, London: Routledge & Kegan Paul.

Withers, H. (1909) *The Meaning of Money* New York: Dutton.

Wojnilower, A.M. (1980) 'The Central Role of Credit Crunches in Recent Financial History' *Brookings Papers on Economic Activity* No. 2, pp. 277–326.

Wojnilower, A.M. (1985) 'Private Credit Demand, Supply and Crunches: How Different Are the 1980s?' *American Economic Review* Vol. 75, No. 2, pp. 351–356.

Wolfson, M. (1999) 'Financial Instability and the Credit Crunch of 1966' *Review of Political Economy* Vol. 11, No. 4, pp. 407–414.

Wood, A. (1975) *A Theory of Profits* Cambridge: Cambridge University Press.

Wray, L.R. (1990) *Money and Credit in Capitalist Economies: The Endogenous Money Approach* Aldershot, UK and Brookfield, VT, USA: Edward Elgar Publishing.

Wray, L.R. (1994) 'The Political Economy of the Current U.S. Financial Crisis' *International Papers in Political Economy* Vol. 1, No. 3, pp. 1–51.

Wray, L.R. (1999) 'The 1966 Financial Crisis: Financial Instability or Political Economy?' *Review of Political Economy* Vol. 11, No. 4, pp. 415–426.

Wray, L.R. (2010) 'Money' *Working Paper* No. 647 December.

Index